INTERNATIONAL TEXTBOOKS IN ART EDUCATION

Italo L. de Francesco, Consulting Editor

GRAPHIC DESIGN

A Creative Approach

GRAPHIC DESIGN

A Creative Approach
By Matthew Baranski

INTERNATIONAL TEXTBOOK COMPANY
SCRANTON 15, PENNSYLVANIA

To My Wife

EDITOR'S PREFACE

Graphic Design as used in this connection refers to works of art which are produced and may be reproduced by the process of imprinting.

The materials and the technics of letterpress, etching, drypoint, block printing, lithography and similar processes furnish a clarification of the meaning intended in Dr. Baranski's book.

The teacher and student of design, or the amateur reader, will find that the author has gathered together, through the experimentation of students in many schools throughout the nation, a vast number of usual and equally vast number of unusual ways of creating design by utilizing surfaces which will "print" or reproduce what has been carved, incised or even scratched upon them. These experiments should open wide new ways of designing for many.

Schopehauer once said that: "It is possible to be at once simple and sublime." Such is the case here as one considers the ordinary nature of the materials suggested to obtain outstanding results.

Good design, on the other hand, goes beyond materials and processes. The latter help, but the *sense* of design is something intangible; it is the unique which each student creates. It is an individual idiom, even when a utilitarian purpose may be served. The author stresses good design as the supreme need in graphic expression.

Ideas are priceless. Yet, the crying need of many in the classroom is for *ideas*. Actually, what they mean is *stimulation*; stimulation from which they progress to express their own ideas. In a sense this book is a basis for stimulation.

Classroom situations of a normal sort, namely the conditions under which most of us have worked or are working, have been utilized by the author. Implicit in this fact is the belief that nearly everyone engaged in teaching art can find in the book ways of enlivening the program.

The illustrations have been carefully chosen from a wide geographic area. This is a further indication of the broad scope of the work and proof that graphic design has wide potentialities as a means of expression.

Altogether, the author has prepared a sound instrument for the use of teachers and pupils who can profit by experimentation as a way toward broader adventures in creative achievement in design.

I. L. de FRANCESCO

FOREWORD

This book deals primarily with the work of students who had experimented and expressed their own thoughts, ideas or feelings with an assortment of materials, tools and various methods of printing, under the guidance of teachers. During these activities of experimenting and creating, pupils learned about design. In short, pupils learned by doing.

The term, graphic, as used in the title, means the art of making lines, solid masses, tones and other marks in such a way that many proofs may be produced from the original block, or stencil, or metal plate.

Objects with unusual shapes, textures or other characteristics, found in nature and man-made objects were used by students at different grade levels to help them understand and appreciate design.

Discovering an assortment of materials with which to experiment, helped the pupils to develop powers of observation and imagination. Pupils learned that there was more than one way of doing things.

Creative ability was developed through the manipulation of materials and tools. Critical judgment was improved through careful selection and evaluation of the materials, tools and methods which pupils used to express their thoughts, ideas and feelings effectively.

Pupils at the junior and senior high school levels were introduced to possible vocations and avocations in the field of graphic design. Many pupils developed technical skills and an appreciation of good craftsmanship. Whenever possible, pupils' work was related to objects used in everyday life. This tended toward making the projects more real and meaningful to the students.

Although many of the methods of printing used by pupils had been experienced before, to many this was a first experience and a discovery. Since it was new to them, it made learning more exciting and motivated them toward further discovery, exploration and creation.

Impressions made from objects found in nature and man-made designs have an historical background that dates back thousands of years. It

1

Cylinder Seal and Impression
Akkadian—C 2500—2200 B.C.
C'sargon of Accad United Mesopotamia
Lapis Lazuli Seal 25 x 17

2

Stamp Seals and
Impressions in Moist
Clay

Photographer
C. E. Simmons

3

4

5

seems to be in the scheme of nature to leave some kind of a record. Scientists have collected and classified valuable information about animal and insect life by studying impressions made in layers of rock and other materials in nature. Leaving an impression or a record in a variety of materials and using different methods has also been a strong desire of people throughout the ages.

Figure 1 shows an example of an Akkadian cylinder seal and impressions dated 2500-2200 B.C. This seal was carved from lapis lazuli. Figure 2 shows stamp seals carved from similar materials and impressions in moist clay.

Interesting impressions have been made by the Chinese from tomb tiles similar to the one shown in Figure 3 which dates back to the Han Dynasty, 206 B.C. — 220 A.D. Rice paper or other soft, absorbent paper was placed over the tile and wetted down with a sponge until the paper molded itself smoothly around the relief figures and in the incised lines. When the paper was dry, an inked dauber was pounded over it. The raised surfaces received more ink and, therefore, appeared darker. When the ink was almost dry the paper was carefully removed and stretched out flat. Figure 4 shows a finished print made in the above described manner.

Movable type designed for printing manuscripts was another method of making impressions. Figure 5 is an example of movable type used in

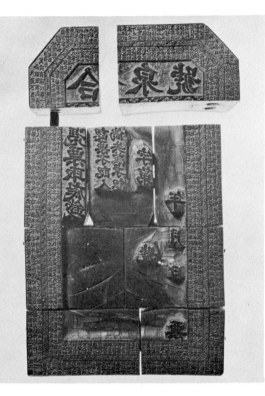

China about 1300 A.D. The type was carved in wood and found in the Cave of Tun-Huang. Figure 6 is an example of a type block which was carved of horn and used in China for printing bank certificates.

Movable type was also used by Gutenberg to print the Bible. Figure 7 is a copy of a page from the Gutenberg Bible. Although there seems to be some controversy as to the date that this Bible was printed, one authoritative source, the Lincoln Library of Essential Information gives the date as being approximately 1455.

A clever arrangement of brass seals designed by a Chinese artist is shown in Figure 8. Each square with five seals fits into another, the largest of the five squares is 1 ⅜ inches.

Self-expression through graphic art provided for the satisfaction of the creative urge of people all over the world through the ages. Today, these same activities of discovering and experimenting with a variety of materials, tools and processes, help to satisfy the creative urge in our students and help to satisfy the restlessness which is characteristic of our school-age population.

These activities offer an opportunity for the students to understand what was done in the past, become aware of contemporary design, and presents a challenge to shape the art of the future.

MATTHEW BARANSKI

ACKNOWLEDGMENTS

This book is the outgrowth of working with many persons in the field of art and related areas of education as well as persons in many walks of everyday life. Hundreds of pupils at the elementary, junior high, high school and college levels have had something to do with this book in one way or another. Much of the work presented has been done under actual classroom experimentation, observation and evaluation.

Special recognition is given to Dr. Stanley Czurles who was most generous in allowing me to use the library facilities and to obtain help from members of the faculty at the State University of New York College for Teachers at Buffalo, New York. Dr. D. Kenneth Winebrenner was most helpful in aiding me in evaluating some of the students' work, clarifying some points related to the philosophy of art education, recent trends, and recommending names of resource, persons and institutions who proved to be most helpful.

Marie Rosso, State Teachers College Campus School, Buffalo, submitted the Christmas card designs and other art work used in this publication. George O'Connell was most cooperative with information pertaining to graphic arts and submitting work of his pupils from different institutions where he taught. Some of his own work was also used.

Sister Magdalen Mary, I. H. M., Immaculate Heart College, Los Angeles, California has graciously given me many photographs of pupils' work. These were most welcome and appreciated.

Jennie Thomas, Holley Central School, Holley, New York contributed a great variety of prints

from different grade levels, which were carefully annotated with appropriate descriptions and explanations. Joanne Lichtenthal, Bowmansville Elementary School presented pupils' work from different grade levels and many of the children who posed for the pictures. Dr. Virginia Cummings, Curator of Anthropology at the Buffalo Museum of Natural Science gave valuable information pertaining to the objects used for the historical background of printing presented in the Forward. She selected and evaluated objects from the Museum collection which best tell the story in a variety of ways.

The Public Relation Section of Birge Co., Inc., Buffalo, New York gave interesting information about printing wallpaper and some fine examples of silk screen panels produced by that company.

Although many students helped with photographing group pictures and projects, two were especially helpful and did a fine job—Gerald Ruth and Dan Terrana, both former students at Buffalo East High School.

The author is most appreciative of the help and encouragement given by his mother, Janina Baranski who spent many hours taking care of his two daughters, Stephanie and Felicia. This book is dedicated to the author's wife, Rita G. Baranski, who spent numerous hours, typing, proofreading and giving of herself the best to help make this book a reality.

Simplest and most varied ways of making a print are through photography. Pupils experience a real thrill watching their designs emerge. Other processes are also intriguing and exciting.

LIST OF ILLUSTRATIONS

Drawings and photographs were submitted from many persons and places. The author is most grateful to the institutions and persons whose names appear after the figure numbers.

Figure	Description or Content	Institution	Artist and/or Photographer
Frontis-piece	Diann Barker	Lafayette H. S. Buffalo, N. Y.	Author
1	Cylinder Seal and Impression	Buffalo Museum of Natural Science Buffalo, N. Y.	C. E. Simmons
2	Stamp Seals	Buffalo Museum of Natural Science Buffalo, N. Y.	C. E. Simmons
3	Tomb Tile	Buffalo Museum of Natural Science Buffalo, N. Y.	C. E. Simmons
4	Imprint from Tomb Tile	Buffalo Museum of Natural Science Buffalo, N. Y.	C. E. Simmons
5	Movable Type	Buffalo Museum of Natural Science Buffalo, N. Y.	C. E. Simmons
6	Type Block	Buffalo Museum of Natural Science Buffalo, N. Y.	C. E. Simmons
7	Page from Gutenberg Bible	Buffalo Museum of Natural Science Buffalo, N. Y.	C. E. Simmons
8	Brass Seals	Buffalo Museum of Natural Science Buffalo, N. Y.	C. E. Simmons
9	Figure in Papier Maché	Immaculate Heart Col. Los Angeles, Calif.	Betty Henderson
10	Intaglio *Throughout This Life*	Courtesy: George O'Connell	Tom Mahoney
11a-c	Diagram of Methods of Printing	—	Author
12	Doodle	Buffalo East H. S. Buffalo, N. Y.	Robert Schultz
13	Christine Baranski	Queen of Martyrs Cheektowaga, N. Y.	Author
14		—	Author
15		—	Author
16		—	Author
17		—	Author
18		—	Author
19		—	Author
20	Hand Print	Buffalo East H. S. Buffalo, N. Y.	James Allen
21		—	Author

GRAPHIC DESIGN

A Creative Approach

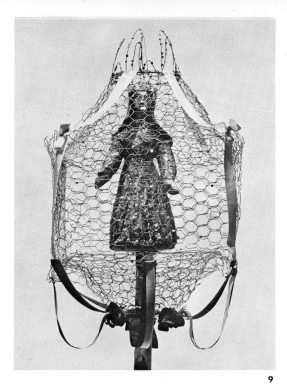

![CHAPTER 1]

The Meaning of Design

There is no one definition of the term design. It has different meanings for different people. To some it may be a scheme, a plan, a composition and arrangement, or the expression of a mood or feeling. To others it may be a pattern as seen in a snowflake. An astrologer may think of design in terms of the solar system; a historian in terms of the pattern created by history repeating itself; a biologist may think of design in terms of life cycles of plants and animals or in terms of patterns formed by bacteria and the structure of bones and tissue. To philosophers design may be a way of life, or life itself.

There are many different types of design: structural construction, functional, geometric, abstract, realistic, and decorative, to mention some. A design may be a combination of these types. For example, the Eiffel Tower is structural design and also, among other things, has a functional value in serving as an observation post. The purpose may be utilitarian or it may be, "the expression of feeling," or a combination of both as pointed out by Sybil Emerson in her book, *Design*. She states: "A chair, for example, may be a comfort-able place to sit. It may also, through its proportions and materials, speak of comfort or elegance or informality or of some other specific quality."[1]

Design may be graphic, printed on flat surfaces, or may be three-dimensional. Figure 9 is an example of three-dimensional design. This means that the object has length, width, and depth, or that it is made in the round. Figure 10 shows a graphic, or two-dimensional, design which has length and width. Some designs that are printed on flat surfaces may appear to have the feeling or to create the illusion of depth or a three-dimensional effect. Basically, there are three methods involved in printing graphic designs as illustrated in Figure 11a, b and c.

Figure 11a is sometimes referred to as planographic and has to do with printing from a flat surface such as a stone in lithography.

Figure 11b is called relief printing; type-set raised letters is an example of this method.

Figure 11c illustrates the intaglio method. When printing with this method, the background makes

[1] Sybil Emerson, *Design—A Creative Approach* (Scranton: International Textbook Co., 1953) p. 3.

the impression and the incised, or cutout, part of the design remains the color of the paper. This is the reverse of the relief, or raised, method.

Design means a different thing to different artists or schools of art. For example, the futurist movement, which began in 1909 against traditionalism, was spear-headed by the poet, Tommaso Marinetti. The futurists saw life in which the visual representation of change and movement found expression in the works of Boccioni, Balla, and Severini. This view was also adopted by contemporary graphic designers. To show the movement of a dog running, a futurist would paint twenty legs instead of painting only four.

The cubists, on the other hand, were concerned with space as well as with representation; in forms, planes, surfaces, and geometrical shapes. This movement was based on the theories of Paul Cézanne.

Suprematists found inspiration in mechanization. They saw design in the flight of an airplane formation or the fields seen from the air.

Another movement, known as the school of neoplasticism, was founded by the poet, Theo Van Doesburg; the painter, Mondrian; the sculptor, Vantongerloo, and the architect, Wells. The abstract forms of painting and sculpture seem to grow out of the geometric layouts of an architect's plan. Mondrian described his work in these words: "By the horizontal-vertical divisions of the rectangle, the neoplasticians obtain tranquility, the balancing of the universe and the individual."

Dadaism, the least understood and perhaps the most ridiculed, was a name given to a movement that revolted against the whole art of painting. The dadaists borrowed a technique of the cubists—papier collés or collages—and pasted up compositions made from scraps of newspaper and other material to create texture. This movement, as well as others, exerted a tremendous influence upon graphic arts. Today we can see the influence of these art movements in everyday objects which are used to furnish our homes: draperies, upholstery material, wallpaper, linoleum tablecloths, rugs, and many others.

Design has a different meaning for different teachers. In *Creative Teaching in Art*, Victor D'Amico points out: "Design is based on such aesthetic values as line, form, color, texture, pattern, and material. Without a sensitiveness to these values a true appreciation of a high standard of production in the arts is not possible."[2]

In *Design*, Sybil Emerson states: "Whatever we are designing, we search for the greatest harmony between the desired expression and the means used, and this harmony is gained through sensitive choices among movements, forms, colors, and materials. We hope for that freedom of imagination which will make the result uniquely our own, bearing the individual signature of the maker, however naive or crude."[3]

D. Kenneth Winebrenner in *Jewelry Making* states: "Designs are formed by moving things around; it is as simple as that. You can start with anything. Every time an idea, an element, or an object is moved you change its position in relation to other ideas, elements, or objects, thus producing a new arrangement or design. Whenever you have produced a satisfactory arrangement of several units or parts, you have created a design, and you have become a designer."[4]

[2] Victor D'Amico, *Creative Teaching in Art*, Scranton: International Textbook Co., 1953.

[3] Sybil Emerson, *Design—A Creative Approach* (Scranton: International Textbook Co., 1953) p. 3.

[4] D. K. Winebrenner, *Jewelry Making as an Art Expression* (Scranton: International Textbook Co., 1953) p. 47.

0

From a teacher's point of view, whatever meaning of design is accepted or conceived, it should be kept in mind that design cannot be taught by rules and formulas even though we realize that certain principles and elements do exist, such as balance, unity, harmony, line, mass, color, texture, and so forth. These principles and elements should not be used slavishly but rather to serve the need of the individual. Dedicated teachers are more concerned with the child than with the art work he produces. They try to look beyond the pupil's results on paper to see if creative growth and development took place within the child as he worked.

In this book we are concerned with design as a creation. "To create," D'Amico states in his article, "What is Creative Teaching?", "then, is to invest a moment, a place, or a thing with the new rank of one's uniqueness, to say it your own way. Being creative means to discover or invent something new, a new organization of things, a new basis for thinking, a new insight into art or a way of living, even only a new expectation. It doesn't have to be new to the world, but new to the person."[5]

The importance of developing a sense of design from the elementary grades on is emphasized by de Francesco[6]: "Pattern, or surface decoration, to be more exact, also takes on new meaning at this stage of development for several reasons, and especially because design offers an avenue of expression closely related to the child's desire to decorate himself. This is true, particularly, on the part of girls; in the case of boys, teachers will note a closer observation and apparent approval of pattern as it appears on girls' dresses, on the wallpaper at home, and on other decorative features in their surroundings in general. It is the natural development of the child's powers of observation and of his great awareness of the details about him. Therefore, design deserves proper attention and ample opportunity at this time." This tendency to create in design should be directed toward making this a better world in which to live.

Although dedicated teachers are primarily concerned with the creative growth and development of children as they design, the finished decorative design as an end in itself can be of value. There are tremendous possibilities for functional improvement of surface appeal and aesthetic value. For example, we can admire a fabric design without being concerned as to whether it helped the growth and development of the child who made it.

In summary, we may say that there are many types of design; there is no one definition of design nor one way to design. In addition, many artists spend a lifetime developing their own ideas and theories about design. We recognize that there exist elements and principles of design which, at best, should be used only as guides. Creativeness has to do with freedom of imagination, uniqueness, expressing one's self in his own way. Finally, a design may be admired for what it is without identifying it with the individual who made it.

[5] Victor D'Amico, *What is Creative Teaching?* School Arts Magazine.

[6] I. L. de Francesco, *Art Education, Its Means and Ends* (New York: Harper and Brothers, 1958), Chapter VIII, pp. 263-64.

11

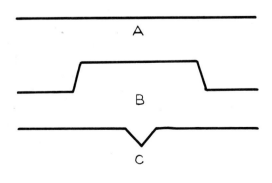

A

B

C

CHAPTER 2

Design and The Child

Today the basic emphasis in art education is on the creative powers of the child rather than on the resulting object.

Because children are different, their art work is different. Each child is an individual with unique creative powers, and adults should respect the creative efforts no matter how naive they look.

Doodles and scribbles are the reflection of a mind at work, a mind that is inquisitive and is exploring. Figure 12 is an example of a doodle design when the pupil was "thinking" with the aid of pen and ink. It shows that the imagination of the individual was functioning. It may be the first of many ideas from which a selection may be made and eventually crystallized into a specific design. Any adverse criticism, ridicule, or belittling of a pupil's efforts serves to hinder the child's natural attempts, gives him a feeling of insecurity and a lack of self-confidence, thus breaking down or thwarting the creative urge to design which is in every child.

Although a child is encouraged to express himself freely, he must at the same time grow socially in his ability to work, play, and get along with others. When encouraging the child to develop his imagination and expression, we are concerned with the whole child and all his senses; the sense of sight, touch, smell, hearing, and taste. It is through these senses that a child learns, grows, and develops. To make sure the child grows and develops, the teacher should have some specific objective in mind so that he may direct the creative efforts of the pupil toward meaningful and worthwhile experiences. These experiences and activities may evolve from situations created in the classroom in which the children took part, or the children and the teacher may discuss a situation or may plan some activity with specific objectives in mind, such as helping to develop greater observation, selecting or making wise choices, obtaining better composition, gaining a greater appreciation of values and texture, be-

coming more skillful in the use of material and tools, or learning how to work and cooperate with others.

It is the teacher's responsibility to see that each child performs in terms of his maximum potentialities. The situations and experiences which the child goes through should be meaningful to him. Each successive activity should become more challenging, disclosing new avenues and paths to further exploration and learning. In this way the child's taste and understanding develops, not only in matters pertaining to the subject matter area and in the school and community, but to the world around him. It is also the responsibility of the teacher to give direction and guidance in such a way that the child develops in creative growth, as well as desirable attitudes, habits, and character; in short, helps him develop a wholesome personality that will make him an acceptable citizen in a democratic society.

The child cannot always conform to adult stand-ards for they may be completely foreign to him. Since children are all different, they will express themselves differently, and their work must be evaluated in terms of individual needs, interests, abilities, creative growth, and understanding of design. These qualities are not easily measured and there are few, if any, standardized tests that are reliable. The teacher must rely on his own observations and judgment and on teacher-prepared tests. A folder of a pupil's work will prove helpful as well as pupil-annotated sketches kept by the teacher. Designs made by students as a class or school project may be evaluated in terms of the aims of the project. To be effective, evaluation must be a continuous process.

Efforts have been made by some educators to make something of a statistical study of behavior patterns, observing specific characteristics of growing individuals at various age levels and sometimes at different grade levels. When one considers the tremendous range in individual differences, it is better to study each child on an individual basis. Start with the child rather than try to fit him into some category or classification. At best, these classifications should be used only as guides.

Through the years the objectives of art education have changed. At one time or another the emphasis was on vocational objectives, art for art's sake, commercial art, history of art, pure aesthetics, and practical art, to mention a few.

The "creative child" is a comparatively new concept. With more emphasis placed on the child rather than on the subject area, an art teacher can no longer be a teacher of a "special subject area," but he must be a person who in addition to his specialty has broad general background in other areas of human development such as psychology, sociology, guidance, and human relations. To understand the creative child, the teacher himself should be able to think, feel, and work creatively.

There was a time when the broad objectives of education centered on the core curriculum, with emphasis placed on the English language or social studies. At other times the emphasis was centered on school activities or the community. In recent years the trend is toward citizenship education and upon the values on which our democratic society is constructed.

In Chapter I, *Human Values in a Democracy*, N.E.A. Third Yearbook, Dr. Edwin Ziegfeld states: "Within the history of free men the need has never been greater to clarify, to define, and to reassert the values upon which the democratic philosophy is based, for the present world conflict is essentially a conflict of values. Our faith in human freedom is challenged by the concept of an all-powerful and infallible state in which the individual is an instrumentality for the realization of the state's absolute power."

Under dictatorial rule, where the state is all-important, indoctrination is employed. The more the individual conforms and obeys, the "nicer" a pupil he is. Under these circumstances, pupils become carbon copies or experts at copying. The emphasis is placed mostly on technical skill instead of exploration and experimentation. Any form of individual expression and freedom of imagination is stamped out. The work lacks spontaneity, has little or no variety, is cold, sterile, stiff and hard, in short, unnatural and mechanical.

Art educators generally agree that the study of design should be considered as part of everyday living in a democratic society and that all children should benefit from it. The less talented students need it so that they may become intelligent consumers, and the talented or gifted children, so that they may become better producers. Society benefits and the world becomes a happier and better place in which to live.

In conclusion, we may point out that emphasis on teaching design, as well as on the aims and objectives of education, has been changing through the years. Today the emphasis is placed on the creative growth of pupils as well as on desirable attitudes and other qualities which will make the pupil an acceptable citizen in a democratic society.

When considering the education of the whole child in terms of these goals, teachers, in addition to their specialized training, will need a broad general background in other areas of human development, such as guidance, psychology, sociology, human relations, and others.

In order to make teaching more effective, the activities must be continuously evaluated in terms of pupils' needs, interests, and other qualities, as well as in terms of the aims and objectives of the project. This may be done by teacher-prepared tests, teachers' observations and judgment, pupils' folders, and annotated sketches. There are few, if any, reliable standardized tests.

Design and related art activities should be made available for all children.

13

CHAPTER 3

Designs Created With Fingers,
Hands, and Varied Materials

Some experiments in this chapter were made by children of different grade levels. They were learning about design through exploring a variety of simple ways of printing. For the most part, the children used their fingers, thumbs, and hands. These experiments were valuable because they helped develop manipulative skills.

The materials used were inexpensive and easily obtained. Some large sheets of absorbent paper, such as unprinted newspaper, were excellent to use. One-inch squared paper, tracing paper, hand-toweling, colored wrapping paper, tissue, and other papers and objects were used by the children. Experimentation with different papers and objects was encouraged.

Stamp pads, the kind that are used in offices, were found most satisfactory for children to use. These stamp pads can be readily appreciated since they are practically unbreakable, no ink can be spilled, and they may be used over and over again. Some companies guarantee their stamp pads for 100,000 impressions. Stamp pads are inexpensive, easy to use, easy to store, and come in various sizes and colors. They eliminate the need of mixing inks and using extra containers and utensils. Prints made by using stamp pads are usually clear and uniform in appearance. When purchasing stamp pads, care should be taken to make sure that the ink used is not poisonous and will not injure or irritate the user's skin. Our experience was that most manufacturers take these factors into consideration. Any laundry or household bleaching agent for removing stains did an excellent job of cleaning the ink from the hands. In our experiments, printers' ink and tempera colors were also used.

By experimenting with their fingers, thumbs, and hands, the children do not have to be concerned with drawing. The emphasis is placed on creative arrangement and application of the process to things he uses in everyday life, whether in or out of school. By comparing his fingerprints with others, the student soon becomes aware that everybody's fingerprints are different. This observation also helps to refresh the instructor's mind that individual differences must be taken into consideration in creative printing when working with children. It points up the fact that each child is different and must be considered on an individual basis.

When working with children, especially at the primary grade level, the instructor should assume a subordinate position and assist and guide the child only if there is a need for it. He should never impose his own ideas on the child and be critical of the pupil's work. The results are not important; what is important is that the child be given an opportunity to do creative work and express himself according to his desires and abilities. The child's work should be evaluated in terms of how meaningful it was to him as an individual. Any copy work, fixed patterns, or rules should be discouraged. The child should be given an opportunity to discover orderly arrangements for himself if he is inclined to do so. The instructor should strive to create in the classroom a permissive atmosphere in which the pupils can express themselves freely. If the student does not seem to understand what he may do, he should be motivated through suggestions in such a way that he may discover for himself what he should do.

Figure 13 shows the method of printing with the thumb after applying the ink from the stamp pad to the thumb by pressing the thumb firmly

14

against the stamp pad. By rolling the thumb from left to right and back again several times, more ink can be applied to the thumb. Before developing any original pattern by printing with the thumb, the students experimented on pieces of scrap paper to make sure that the thumb prints

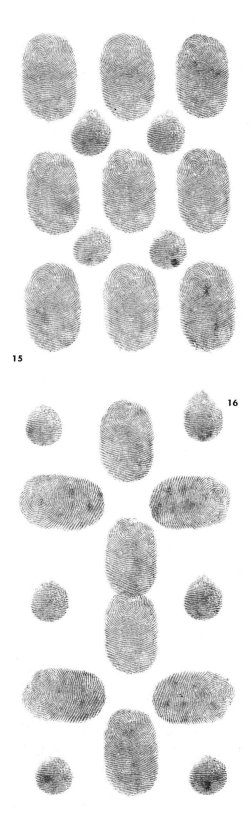

15

16

were of the same value. It was noticed that several tries had to be made before the thumb absorbed sufficient ink to make prints of similar value.

To get acquainted with this simple process of printing, only the thumb was used, as shown in Figure 14. If an orderly arrangement is desired by the pupil, one-inch squared paper may be used. The student may use the squares to guide him. Some children discovered that by fastening a piece of tracing paper over the one-inch squared paper with pieces of transparent tape, the squared lines were clearly seen through the tracing paper and could be used as a guide when the printing was done on the tracing paper.

Some pupils discovered different and more interesting arrangements by using the thumb and the tip of a finger to print with, as shown in Figures 15 and 16. Other pupils found that they could print with three or four fingertips simultaneously, as illustrated in Figure 17. Still others discovered that they could use the side of the thumb, as shown in Figures 18 and 19.

One pupil at the junior high school level used his hand to print the over-all design shown in Figure 20. An examination of the handprint disclosed that the fingers seemed to radiate from the base of the palm. Radiation is common in nature forms. Sometimes radiation may be from a straight or a curved line as seen in a fish skeleton or a leaf. It may also be from a point as, for example, in a wheel or a flower like a daisy.

It was also noted that the middle finger was the longest and the fingers on each side were gradually a little shorter. Thus, gradation was discovered. Another example of gradation of size can be seen in a fern.

Figures 21, 22, 23, and 24 show different textural effects produced by placing different kinds of cloth over the thumb and then printing with it. The ink drawings in Figure 25 show the use of the thumb in different positions as observed in many of the children's prints. These are but a few examples.

Figure 26 shows the thumb and finger printing process applied to paper toys, a book cover design and Christmas tree decorations. Figure 27

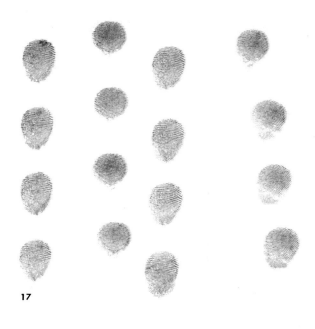

17

to him has completed her design with paint and is ready to place a piece of paper right on top of the paint. Finally, the last boy is shown completing a print.

Figure 29 shows some interesting results which were obtained by the pupils. It was soon discovered that color combinations of contrasting values had the greatest carrying power and could be seen more clearly at a greater distance. See if you can pick out the design which has the greatest carrying power of those shown in Figure 29. Figure 30 is a colored reproduction of one of these prints. In Figure 30 it was discovered that varied line thicknesses and a variety of shapes added interest to a design. There is an old adage which states that variety is the spice of life.

Figure 31 shows another variation of the monoprint made by a junior high school pupil. (Monoprints were made by pupils from grades 1 to 12.) Instead of dropping the tempera colors directly on the glass, as previously mentioned, the glass was first painted with a large brush and as soon as

gives an idea of another way Easter eggs may be decorated. The eggs, as well as many of the other objects shown in this chapter, were printed with many different colors. These experiments were made by students in grades 1 to 3.

Students beyond these grades may become acquainted and may experiment with simple ways of printing by making monoprints. The materials used for monoprints are: a piece of glass, tempera or showcard paint, and a variety of different colored and textured paper. In experimenting with this method, we tried to have the children work freely, using their imaginations in such ways as to create original designs. We also tried to help them understand something about interesting color combinations.

Figure 28 shows junior high school pupils experimenting with monoprints. These prints are referred to as monoprints since only one print can be made by using this method. In Figure 28 we see the first boy on the right applying showcard paint directly to a piece of glass, approximately 9 by 12 inches, in a very free manner. Fingers or a mixing stick may be used. The boy used several different colors which harmonized. The girl next

18

possible, different colors were spattered on with the fingers while the background was still wet. The print was then made as previously described. The blending of the spattered color with the background color seemed to create a different feeling or mood. The misty, dream-like effect, with the indefinite shapes, is very stimulating to the viewer's imagination. Some of these prints make excellent wall hangings; others may serve as ideas for further development of textile designs.

To summarize, we may say that learning to manipulate with the fingers is very important for pupils who want to express themselves through art activities. Experiments with finger and thumb printing give pupils an excellent opportunity to improve manipulating skills.

In these simple printing experiments we discovered that by using our imaginations we could produce a great variety of exciting designs and interesting color combinations, and we could ap-

19

20

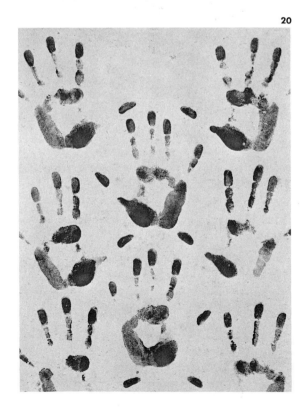

ply design to objects used in everyday life. We discovered that because persons are different, they produce different designs so that no two designs are alike. We also discovered that designs may be carefully planned to form an orderly pattern, or they may be free and spontaneous in appearance.

Simple ways of doing things are sometimes the most direct and easily understood. By using their thumbs and fingers, a stamp pad, a piece of glass, and tempera colors, the children discovered what a challenge and delightful experience printing is. For some it was an outlet for emotional tension. For others it was an opportunity to discover how to make more effective use of their hands. Other children had their curiosity and interest aroused and thus became more observant. Still others gained some appreciation of order. For some it

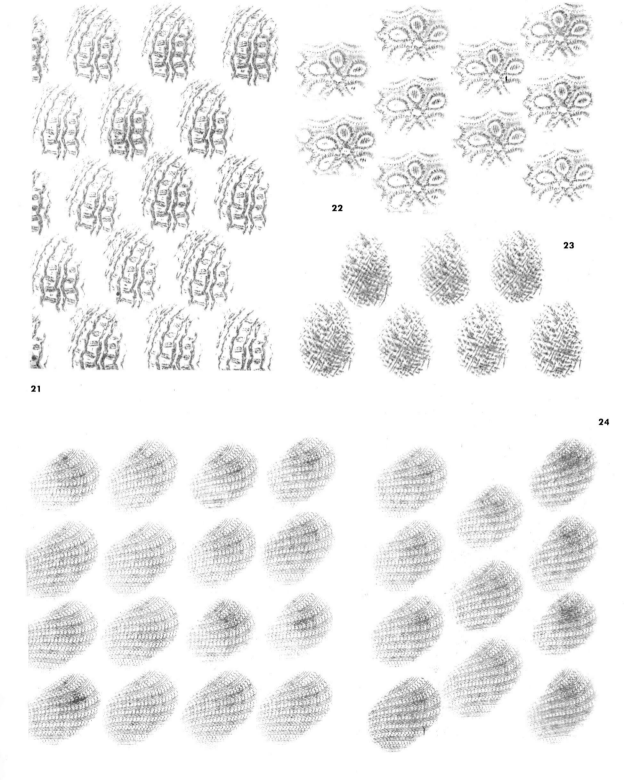

21

22

23

24

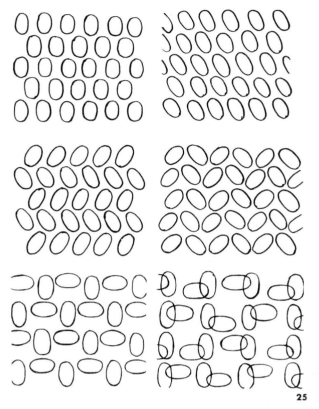

25

was a real and meaningful experience which helped stimulate their imaginations and started them exploring many more different ways of printing. All these activities began with the interest and desires of the child, within the range of his own abilities. Pupils began to enlarge their

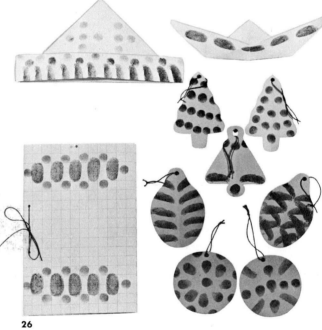

26

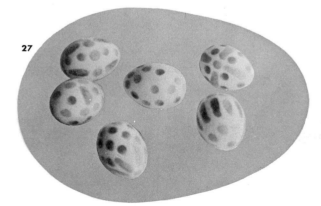

27

vocabularies and to get some idea of the meaning of radiation, gradation, texture, carrying power, and variety of shapes.

The work of the children was evaluated in terms of their own needs and interests and how much they as individuals learned through these experiments. Of course, some designs appealed more to the group of children than others. The children looked at the designs to determine whether they liked them or not and whether or not the design served the purpose for which it was intended.

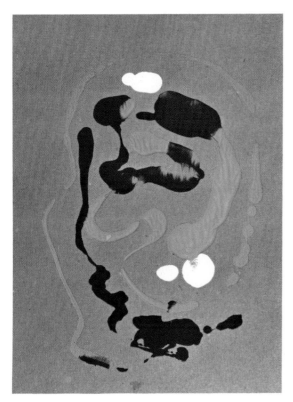

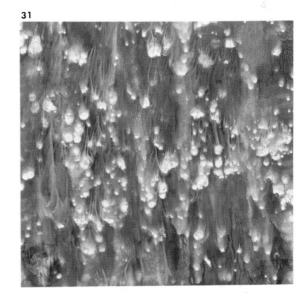

A word of caution to teachers:

This chapter, as well as the other chapters in this book, is a record of prints by students and of how they apply to different types of objects used in everyday life. Do not permit these ideas to be copied. At best, they should be used only as suggestions to get the pupils to start exploring and discovering new and different ways of printing to help them gain a better understanding of design. Your pupils will benefit most from using their imagination to create their own designs and to develop their own methods of printing.

CHAPTER 4

Designs Created With Kneaded Erasers and Plasticene

Every child likes to work with his hands. This was especially true when a piece of kneaded eraser was handed to him. Whether it was the pupil's first experience with the eraser or whether he had used it previously, there was no end to the fascination it held. Because the kneaded eraser is plastic, it provided the children with many opportunities to form different shapes; to understand a little more about design; and to become acquainted with another way of printing.

The materials used were kneaded erasers, plasticene, pieces of corrugated paper, printing inks, **tempera** colors or a stamp pad, a roller, and

a brush. A kneaded eraser is sometimes referred to as a charcoal eraser since charcoal is one of the art mediums with which this type of eraser is used. Kneaded erasers are inexpensive and may be obtained in almost any store which handles art materials. This eraser fascinates children and adults alike because it is pliable. It may be shaped and reshaped. It retains its shape, it is clean, it has no objectionable odor, and it has a pleasant "feel" to it. In the hands of an individual it becomes a challenge. When the eraser is held in the palm of the hand, and the warmth of the body makes it soft and pliable, the first impulse is to squeeze, shape, and reshape the eraser into all kinds of forms to satisfy one's curiosity and imagination.

Before actually attempting to make a design, the students experimented with the material to get acquainted with it. They rolled, stretched, twisted, pinched, curled, waved, flattened, pointed, rounded, folded, cut, and incised with a knife or a pair of scissors. Figure 32 shows a 4th grade student rolling the eraser and making a "worm."

In order to print with the kneaded eraser designs, it proved helpful for some students to fasten the design to a rigid backboard. It was soon discovered that corrugated cardboard answered the purpose very well. Pieces of corrugated cardboard, approximately 2 inches by 2 inches, were cut out of boxes obtained from a grocery store. Although large scissors or a paper cutter do a good job of cutting the cardboard, a pair of large tin snips proved to be the best all-around cutting tool.

33

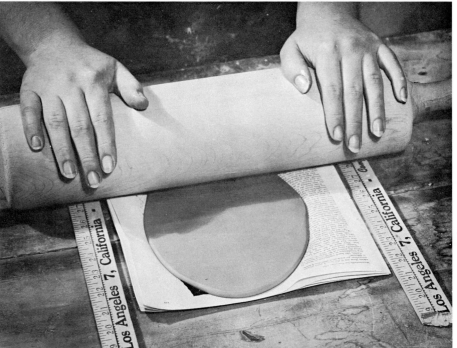

After the corrugated cardboard was cut to the approximate size, each piece was coated with rubber cement, which was applied with a brush. If the cement was too thin, the cardboard pieces were given a second coat. After selecting the best kneaded eraser design, the underside of the design was coated with rubber cement and put aside to dry for a few seconds. The design was then picked up gently, turned over, and placed carefully in the center of the prepared cardboard. A book was then placed on the design and a little pressure applied to help secure the kneaded eraser to the cardboard and to flatten the design so that it would print evenly.

Figure 33 shows another way which was used to flatten out plasticene to use it the same way as a kneaded eraser. By using two rulers and a rolling pin, uniformity of thickness was assured. This method was useful when making larger designs and when using several pieces of kneaded eraser.

By gluing the kneaded eraser or plasticene design on the piece of cardboard, we had a raised surface with which to print. This is sometimes referred to as relief printing and is one of the three basic methods used in printing which were discussed in the chapter dealing with design.

Sometimes a combination of the relief and the intaglio methods may be used in the same design. Figure 34 is an example of this combination made by a junior high school pupil. This same solid, or mass, design was used for the over-all pattern in Figure 35.

34

35

Figure 36 shows some variations of a "worm" made by an elementary pupil. One of these "worms" was mounted on a piece of corrugated cardboard and formed into a helix. Figure 37 is an example of an over-all pattern created by holding the kneaded eraser stamp in different positions when printing.

The following things were observed before and during printing. First, we inspected the kneaded eraser design to see that it was securely fastened to the cardboard. Then, the design was applied to the stamp pad several times to give the eraser an opportunity to absorb a sufficient amount of ink.

Figure 38 shows a girl in the 9th grade applying tempera paint to a design with a brush instead of using a stamp pad. In some instances, a roller was satisfactorily used.

As in the previous chapter, a piece of 9 by 12 inch tracing paper was fastened with paper clips to one-inch squared paper. The squared paper lines were used as a guide when printing on the tissue paper. Different colors were used. When printing, the students were careful to hold the cardboard straight and level and, when applying the kneaded eraser stamp to the paper, they were sure that the fingertips did not touch the tissue paper, for they might have been stained with ink and would have left undesirable impressions on the paper. With a little practice, satisfactory over-all prints were made without using guides.

Since some of the designs used for printing with kneaded erasers are line designs, it may be pointed out that some lines, as shown in Figure 39, give the feeling of movement and action. Other lines, as shown in Figure 40, show force. Those in Figure 41 show grace, and those in Figure 42 show mystery.

Solid, or mass, designs made with kneaded erasers may be nonrepresentative or abstract, as shown in Figure 43. This design is reminiscent of ink-blot designs. Or, they may be naturalistic as the fish design shown in Figure 44.

Some of these designs may be used for wall decorations, toys, wrapping paper, tiles, textile designs, plastic curtains, and tablecloths.

CORRUGATED PAPER

KNEADED ERASER

36

37

In evaluating kneaded eraser prints made by the students, emphasis was placed on the importance of new and different designs, and how well the students expressed their ideas.

Designs made by the use of kneaded erasers must be simple and bold since this material does not adapt itself to detailed and intricate designs. Understanding the material and how to use it effectively is an important consideration.

In summary, we can say that plastic materials, because of their physical properties, make for a great variety of shapes. They are stimulating to the imagination since they can be shaped and reshaped with ease. As with many other materials used for printing, good workmanship in preparing the stamp must be stressed.

When using a kneaded eraser, line designs as well as solid, or mass, designs can be made. Solid designs may be incised to add interest; however, simple, bold designs are usually best. Paint or ink may be applied by using a stamp pad, a roller, or a brush.

Designs may be, among other things, abstract or naturalistic. They may also suggest force, grace, mystery, or action.

38

We rediscovered the design form of the helix which can be seen in plant, animal, and marine life. A conical sea shell is an example of a helix design. We learned and employed two of the basic methods of printing—relief and intaglio.

The teacher should exercise caution in storing the finished stamps. Design stamps should be stored face up and should rest on the corrugated cardboard. Under no circumstances should one stamp be stored on top of another since the material is soft and pliable. Temperature and the amount of pressure exerted on the kneaded eraser and plasticene stamp may affect the design.

39

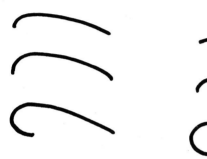

40

41

42

43

44

CHAPTER 5

Designs Created With Sponges

The experiments in this chapter had to do with using sponges for printing. Since sponges are on the bulky side, they are a good material to use in creating designs in mass rather than line. They are excellent for printing over-all surface designs with unusual textural effects.

The materials used in these experiments were sponges which are commonly found in an office for the purpose of moistening stamps, gummed paper, envelopes, and other things which need to be sealed or held in place with glue. Sponges that were normally used for household purposes were also utilized. To make it more interesting, sponges of different sizes were used, as shown in Figure

45. In addition to the sponges, different kinds of stamp pads, tempera paints, absorbent paper of all kinds, one-inch squared paper, manila paper, and tissue paper were used.

Printing with sponges is especially useful in making surface prints on large pieces of paper, walls, and other large areas. Wrapping paper can be made more decorative quickly and easily by using this method of printing. Decorative patterns may be printed on flat as well as on round or curved surfaces and on all kinds of materials. One pupil decorated a large rubber balloon by using this method and got excellent results. Some pupils printed large border designs on pieces of wrapping paper and used them to decorate the room. Instead of using stamp pads, they used showcard or tempera colors.

Here is the way we got started. Before applying the sponges to the stamp pad or paint, they were first soaked in water, squeezed out, and then placed on a piece of blotting paper to remove the excess water. As a result, the sponges were moist and pliable and when applied to the stamp pad they absorbed the ink more quickly and uniformly.

It was soon discovered that before a sharp and uniform print could be made, it was necessary to practice on a separate piece of drawing paper to give the sponge enough time to absorb the desired amount of ink. Darker prints could be made by pressing a little harder on the sponge. However, if the sponge was pressed too hard, the print came out blurred. It was soon learned that sharp, dark, uniform prints were the result of having the right amount of ink on the sponge, holding

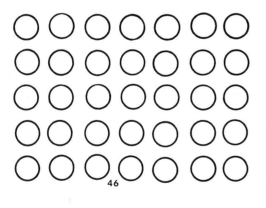

46

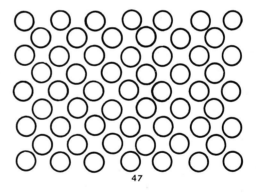

47

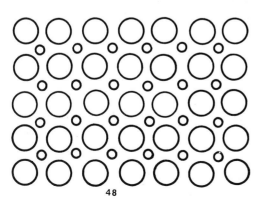

48

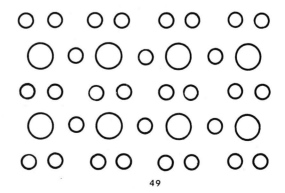

49

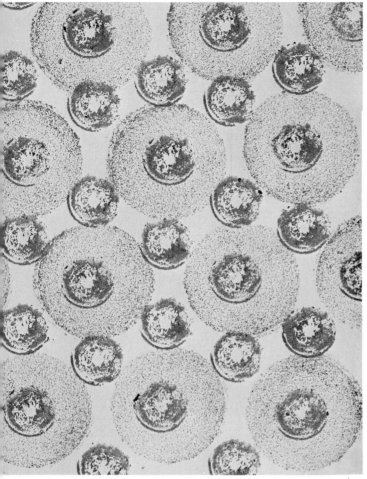

50

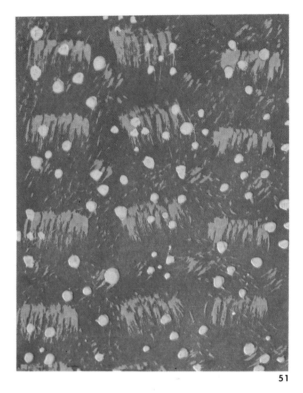

51

52

the sponge in a straight and level position, and consistently applying the same amount of pressure.

In making surface patterns there were many ways of making the prints more interesting as shown in Figures 46, 47, 48, and 49. Figure 46 is a simple surface pattern which may be used, but it is monotonous, regimented, and mechanical. In Figure 47 the pattern is somewhat more interesting because the units were arranged a little differently. In Figure 48 the pattern was made still a little more interesting by changing the arrangement and varying the size

54

56

55

of the units. In Figure 49, interest was brought about by varying the arrangment, size, and grouping of units.

Surface patterns were also made more interesting by making some of the units darker and others lighter, as shown in the surface pattern in Figure 50. This idea was worked out by a 4th grade pupil. Different kinds of sponges produce different kinds of textural effects which also add interest to the design. The same sponges will print differently on different kinds of paper, as well as on different textured wall surfaces. Using color is another way of adding interest to the surface patterns. Interesting results may also be obtained by changing the shape of the sponge by cutting, tearing, or squeezing it when printing.

Boys and girls in grades 3 to 5 did sponge printing at their desks on 9 by 12 inch tissue paper. A simple way to get started was to attach a piece of 9 inch by 12 inch tracing paper to a sheet of one-inch squared paper with paper clips. The lines of the squared paper were visible through the tracing paper and were used as guide lines when the print was done on the tissue paper. Before actual printing was started with the inked sponge, it was advisable to visualize a pattern to follow. Some students who had difficulty visualizing took a piece of cardboard and cut out the shape of their sponges. They removed or raised the tissue paper from the squared paper, placed the cardboard patterns on the squared paper, and moved the patterns around to see how many different kinds of combinations they could create. After they selected the surface patterns which they liked best, they went around the cardboard patterns with a pencil and laid out the complete surface pattern. The tissue paper was replaced over the squared-paper layout, and they were ready to print.

After a little practice, some pupils preferred to print directly with sponges dipped in tempera paint or printing ink, without the use of guide lines. Figures 51 and 52 are examples of the work of a 5th grade student. Figure 53 shows two junior high school boys who were practicing to get the "feel" of the sponge. Figures 54, 55, and 56 are examples of their warm-up exercises. Many of these exercises were interesting because they were simple, direct, and spontaneous, and the rough ideas were later developed and refined. Some pupils preferred to get their ideas in this way; others had a tendency to develop their ideas more systematically, using the step-by-step method. The simple, direct approach was encouraged because the designs usually turned out less rigid and stiff and seemed to reflect the personality of the student a great deal more.

Figure 57 is an example of work done by a student in junior high school. In this experiment he used an old sponge that had been used as a floor mop and another piece of torn sponge. Figure 58 is the work of a 9th grade pupil. A sponge was cut into several pieces of different size. These pieces were dipped into tempera paint to produce this interesting design. In comparing Figure 57 with Figure 58, it is seen that the design in Figure 57 follows a definite pattern whereas the design in Figure 58 is more "free." With its indefinite shapes Figure 58 seems to convey a feeling of movement.

Some applications of sponge printed designs could be in wall decorations, wrapping paper, floor coverings, and textile designs.

When looking at the results of their work to determine what makes a good design, many pupils agreed that originality should rank high on the list. Some pupils examined the design to see how effectively the designer used the materials and tools he had to work with to produce the design. Although the materials used by the pupils were the same in most cases, we all agreed that the techniques varied with each individual. After some time, it was not difficult to identify each pupil with his work.

In summarizing our efforts, we reached the conclusion that printing with sponges adapts itself to making mass designs rather than line designs. We discovered that interesting textural effects can be produced by cutting or tearing the sponge. Surface designs made with sponges can follow an orderly arrangement or can be free and of an indefinite shape. These designs can convey a feeling of movement and have the power to suggest and to stimulate the viewer's imagination.

Printing with sponges gave quick, satisfying results to individuals at practically all age and grade levels.

We learned that surface patterns can be made more interesting by varying the arrangement, size, and grouping of units.

Although there may be some value in learning how to manipulate materials and tools, understanding design is much more than busy work. Teachers should see to it that each experiment and lesson is so planned and guided that the students grow and develop in their appreciation of good design.

57

58

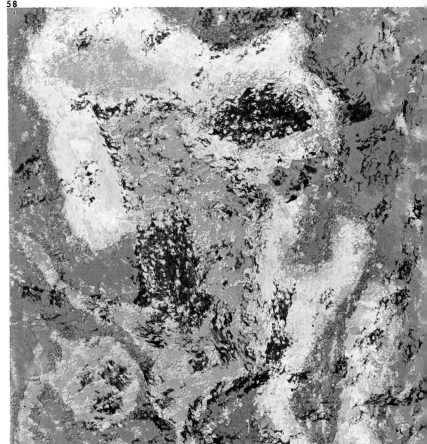

CHAPTER 6

Designs Created With Pipe Cleaners

Pipe cleaners have been used for all kinds of art work. There seems to be no end to their adaptability for creative expression. As with most of the materials used in this book, the pipe cleaners were inexpensive, easily obtainable, and a lot of fun to work with. They were excellent for use in printing because many fascinating and exciting designs could be created. Pipe cleaners were easy to work with and could be bent and shaped into a variety of forms without the use of any special tools. Shaping designs out of pipe cleaners offered an excellent opportunity for the pupils to learn to appreciate lines in art and nature, for it was only through seeing them that this apprecia-

tion was possible. Appreciation of lines was increased by producing lines. Some pupils learned to appreciate lines by drawing with a pencil and then forming the pipe cleaners along those lines. Others preferred working directly with the pipe cleaners. It was found that beautiful lines may be observed in the painting, sculpture, and architecture of all periods of art history.

Materials which were used for printing with pipe cleaners included an ordinary pair of scissors which proved successful in cutting the pipe cleaners, corrugated cardboard, rubber cement, block printing ink, a spatula, a roller, a piece of glass approximately 9 by 12 inches, India ink, a water-

60

color brush for applying the India ink to the design, and some clean rags. Figure 59 and Figure 60 show some of the materials needed for simple experiments in line and solid designs made with pipe cleaners.

Birds, animals, fish, and flowers are excellent subjects to think about when planning a design.

61

One need not necessarily choose many subjects. Sometimes only one subject, such as a bird, may be developed into many variations, as shown in Figure 61. Many of these designs were doodle-designs made by junior high school pupils. When designing, the students were not interested in copying or making a representation of a specific bird; rather, they thought in terms of birds in different positions and activities. Some pupils, impressed with Chinese and Japanese prints, tried to express themselves in such a way as to get the most possible action with the greatest economy of strokes of the pen, pencil, or crayon.

Some pipe cleaner manufacturers make their product in many colors. The pupils found it interesting to choose the most appropriate color for the kind of bird they were designing or the activity the bird was engaged in. A strutting rooster, for example, was made with a red-colored pipe cleaner. It seemed that color actually stimulated the imaginations of the students. A reclining bird was made with a blue pipe cleaner.

Some children are more interested in drawing human beings, especially faces. Drawing the human face is an exciting experience for there are no two faces that are exactly alike. By drawing one another's faces the students got to know and understand one another better. Human faces also make excellent designs for printing. When drawing the face for a design to be used for printing, or when actually working directly with the pipe cleaners the pupils tried to visualize the human head as an oval. They thought in terms of large, simple shapes and forgot about any small details. It was difficult to get an exact likeness of anyone. However, the pupils got enjoyment and satisfaction out of their work by creating the design so that it suggested the individual rather than by making a faithful copy or reproduction. One way of suggesting what the person looked like was to make a caricature of him. This was accomplished by studying the individual's features and discovering some prominent or characteristic shape that identified the person. It may be the forehead, eyes, nose, mouth, chin or ears, or a combination of these features. However, one feature was made more pronounced than any other.

Figure 62 shows three examples of caricatures that would make good designs for printing.

Figure 63 is an over-all print made by a 5th grade pupil. This design was created by experimenting directly with the pipe cleaner. In this experiment the pupil used a pocket-sized mirror to help him develop the design. After making several bends in the pipe cleaner, he placed it next to the mirror. The design was laid flat on the table, and the mirror was placed in a vertical position, or at a 90° angle, to the design. The reflection of the design in the mirror completed the design. Later on it was explained to the pupil that he now had a formal design since both halves were the same. This design was compared with the over-all design shown in Figure 64. This is a simple line design and may be referred to as informal. When the student divided the duck design in half by folding, he discovered that the two halves were not identical. As a matter of fact, they were quite different.

The first step after the pupils shaped their designs with the pipe cleaners was to find some suitable rigid material on which they could mount their designs and prepare them for printing. Masonite, plywood, and cardboard were used by many pupils. Most children liked cardboard, especially corrugated cardboard, because it was the easiest to cut. The pipe cleaner designs were fastened with rubber cement to the corrugated

62

64

cardboard pieces which were cut to approximately a two-inch square. This was done in the same manner as described in a previous chapter.

Instead of using stamp pads, block printing ink was rolled over the design with a roller. This method was selected because the children who were working on this project were in the intermediate grades and could handle these tools and materials. This also provided an opportunity for the boys and girls to enjoy and become acquainted with more tools and materials.

Block printing ink comes in various colors. Some of these inks have an oil base and require turpentine or some other solvent for thinning. These block printing inks are somewhat messy to use and cleaning up the materials and tools becomes quite a problem. The oil-base block printing inks have value in that they are more permanent because they are waterproof. There are also a number of excellent water-soluble block printing inks which simplify the problem of printing and cleaning up.

After inspecting to see that the pipe cleaner designs were securely fastened on the cardboard, they were ready to apply the ink. They squeezed out approximately an inch of the ink in the center of a plate which was either tin or glass, approximately 9 by 12 inches. With a spatula they spread out the ink until it was evenly and smoothly distributed over most of the plate. They took their

65

rollers and went over the ink, back and forth, then side to side. Next, they inspected the roller to see that the ink was evenly distributed on it. The ink was then applied to the design by holding the design right side up between the thumb and index finger. The design stamp and roller were held straight and level and an even pressure was applied to the roller. Care was taken not to get

ink on the backboard. The pupils practiced printing with their design stamps on pieces of scrap
paper until they mastered this technique of printing. Plenty of clean rags came in handy when
working.

In order to place their design stamp in the
right spaces, the pupils squared off the surfaces
with white chalk or charcoal, depending on
whether the paper was dark or light. When the
printing was finished and dried, they dusted the
chalk or charcoal off.

When printing on transparent paper, such as
tissue paper, a sheet of one-inch squared paper
was placed under the tissue and the squared paper lines were used as guide lines.

Line designs may be based on animal forms,
leaves, and human faces, as illustrated in this chapter. They may also be made with geometric forms
such as a square, rectangle, circle, and oval. Figure 65 is an example of a geometric design made
by a junior high school pupil. This over-all pattern
was carried out in two colors. A separate design
was made for each color. Although the pipe cleaner designs were printed on paper, they appear
as if they were printed on cloth.

As pointed out in the beginning of the chapter,
solid designs may also be made with pipe cleaners. When making solid, or mass, designs, one
length of a pipe cleaner was not enough so they
were joined together. Two pipe cleaners were
placed side by side and the ends twisted together
approximately three times about one-half inch
down. The pipe cleaners were then stretched out
and the twisted part flattened out.

Figure 66 shows a variety of over-all solid designs made by junior high school pupils. It was discovered that by spiraling and bending the pipe cleaners one next to the other, a solid mass design could be created. Free forms were used. Although they may suggest many different things to the observer, they do not really look like any specific object. These designs were mounted on corrugated cardboard in the same way as those used for line designs. The pupils printed these designs directly on the tissue paper without guide lines. They used their "eye" to determine the proper intervals. Before printing, the pupils applied India ink with a medium-sized brush over the pipe cleaner design.

Figure 67 is an over-all design pattern created by a 1st grade pupil. In this experiment the child dipped the pipe cleaner into tempera paint and printed directly on the paper.

67

Pipe cleaner designs may be applied to curved surfaces, as shown in Figure 68. A junior high school pupil made this design. In this case the object was a lamp shade. After applying the ink to the pipe cleaner stamp, the student carefully placed it next to the unit previously printed and along a guide line which was lightly drawn around the lamp shade. When printing, one hand was placed inside the lamp shade to assist in applying the pressure to insure a clear and sharp print. Some pupils used this technique of printing to make simple, interesting greeting cards; others made large name plates. Some pupils decorated large paper shopping bags, while still others decorated large sheets of colored tissue paper which they used for wrapping paper.

All pupils should be encouraged to find application of their art experiences to objects in everyday life. By doing so, art becomes a real part of our daily living.

When evaluating the work of the pupils, we asked ourselves why we liked a certain design. We also tried to determine whether or not the design as applied to an object was appropriate. Many pupils liked unusual designs, interesting arrangements, and designs that suggested movement or had a certain "feel" to them.

To summarize the work covered in this chapter, we could readily see that the designs created by printing with pipe cleaners were quickly and easily made because of the nature of the material. These designs could be line or solid. We learned that a design can be formal or informal and that the informal designs seem to be less rigid and may suggest movement whether the design is line or solid.

Interesting designs may be created, and although they may not represent anything specific, they may suggest many things to the viewer.

We also observed that color seems to help stimulate the pupils' imagination when creating designs. Pipe cleaner over-all patterns may be printed in two or more colors. Whether printed in color or with black ink, the design appears as if printed on cloth because the impression made by the pipe cleaner stamp is soft and sometimes fuzzy.

Pupils at almost any school level can print with pipe cleaners. They will enjoy the many creative opportunities offered by doing so.

CHAPTER 7

Designs Created With Foam Rubber

Handling many different kinds of materials that could be used for printing awakens one's imagination to explore further the possibilities of using still other materials. One of the materials which aroused our curiosity was foam rubber.

In this chapter we are going to describe some experiments and experiences encountered when working with foam rubber. Through experimentation we explored the most effective ways to use this material and discovered ways of making designs more interesting.

Foam rubber is gentle to the touch. It is soft and springy, clean, and can be cut easily with a pair of ordinary scissors as shown in Figure 69. It was

inexpensive since only the scraps of foam rubber were needed. Scrap pieces of foam rubber may be obtained from army surplus stores, upholstering establishments, and sometimes in the 5¢ & 10¢ stores, since it is also used as a sponge for washing, in bath mats, and as seat cushions. We were able to obtain small foam rubber pads, approximately 2 ½ by 3 by ¼ inch from the surplus store at a nominal cost. These pads proved to be an excellent size for the boys and girls to work with at their desks.

Figure 70 shows some of the materials and tools that were required in order to print successfully with foam rubber stamps. In addition to ordi-

70

nary scissors, which did an excellent job of cutting the foam rubber, a pair of pinking shears were appreciated by many children, especially for cutting out tree designs.

71

In teaching the children to design in foam rubber, the teacher trained the pupils to think in terms of mass instead of line since this material lends itself to this manner of making designs. Working with foam rubber was a good way to get the children acquainted with this element of design. To help the young folks visualize objects in terms of mass, it was found to be a good idea to have them observe the shadow of their hand on a piece of paper. Other objects were held in the direct rays of the light against a white background and the shadow or silhouette of the object was then pointed out to the pupils. In one class experiment, the students made fine silhouettes of each others' heads, using the above method. When the head was silhouetted against a sheet of white paper, one of the pupils traced around it with a pencil. This white sheet was placed over a black sheet of paper and the two were cut out together. The result was a white and a black silhouette. These silhouettes were then pasted on a sheet of gray paper.

Another ingenious way to help pupils think in terms of mass designs was to have them fold pieces of 2 by 2 inch white drawing paper in half, open it and place a drop of ink in the fold or a little to the left or right of the fold, and then fold and place the two halves of the paper together again. When the paper was opened, a surprisingly unusual design was formed.

The children also observed silhouettes in nature and man-made objects out of doors, especially at sunset. Distant objects on land, in the sky, and on the water appear as silhouettes too.

72

73

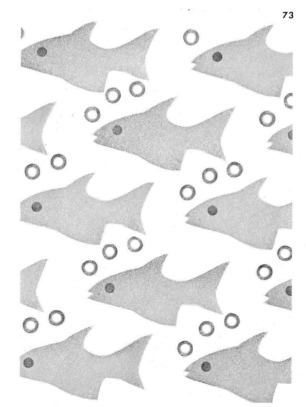

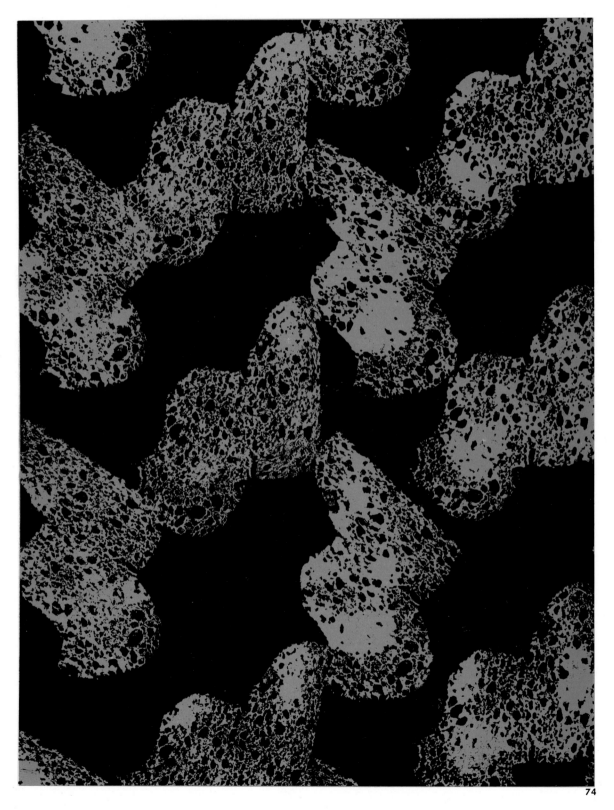

Getting the boys and girls in this frame of mind seemed to gear them to a state of readiness when they began to create their own mass designs. As with other materials, some students worked out simple bold designs in crayon or soft pencils; others preferred to work directly by cutting into the foam rubber with a pair of scissors. Where the direct method was preferred and the supply of foam rubber was limited, the pupils practiced cutting designs out of cardboard or construction paper. These were then traced on the foam rubber with a soft wax crayon and the designs were cut out with a scissors.

As with other materials discussed in the previous chapters, some of the foam rubber cutouts were fastened to two-inch squares of corrugated cardboard. Colored stamp pads, water-soluble block printing ink, tempera colors, a metal or glass plate, a spatula, clean rags, drawing paper, colored tissue paper, and paper hand toweling were some of the materials and tools used. When using office stamp pads, quicker and better results were obtained if the foam rubber design stamps were slightly moistened with water.

Figure 71 shows an example of place cards made by pupils in the 6th grade, using the foam rubber printing technique. White drawing paper was used for this project. However, colored construction paper may also be used. When making these place cards, a piece of 9 by 12 inch white drawing paper was creased in half and cut. The half sheets were again folded, creased, and cut. In short, four pieces of paper were cut from the 9 by 12 inch drawing paper. These pieces were again folded in half and printed. By opening the place cards a little bit, they could be made to stand upright.

The design for these place cards was a simple tree. To add texture, pinking shears were used to cut around the design. In this particular project the foam rubber stamp design was inked with a roller, using black, water-soluble ink. The names were first written in pencil, then inked with a No. 3 round-nibbed pen. This is only one way of making place cards by using the foam rubber technique of printing. It is not intended that the reader will copy the design since the emphasis throughout this book is placed on creative printing which implies that you create and develop your own projects.

The small circles in the upper right-hand corners of the place cards were printed with a piece of rubber hose that fitted over a pencil.

Sometimes one design, with a little variation, may be used again for another project, as shown in Figure 72. This over-all design was made by a boy to be used for a Christmas book cover design. The ornaments were printed over the tree design with a pencil eraser. The over-all pattern in Figure 73 was made by a junior high school girl for a wallpaper design to be used in a doll house. The rubber hose and pencil eraser which were used in other designs were combined and used appropriately for this wallpaper design.

It will be noted that the designs in Figures 72 and 73 are simple silhouette cutouts. The designs were made a little more interesting with the addition of subordinate units of design created with a hose and pencil. Dominance and subordination are important factors in some designs.

Figure 74 is an example of a print made by a junior high school pupil. It is a nonrepresentative type of design and interesting results were obtained by changing the position of the design while printing. The foam rubber which was used by the student was of a coarse type, with larger and more varied pores, which seems to add to the design.

Figure 75 shows some silhouette designs which are variations of bird, butterfly, tree, and fish designs. These designs were made by a junior high school pupil. These variations are but a few that were made by either widening or narrowing some part of the design or by changing the general shape a little. These examples are shown to give some idea of the advantage of working in a flexible manner when designing, for by having many designs, a selection can be made. There is no one way of making a design, but rather, many and varied ways. To be more exact, there are as many ways and different kinds of designs as there are people who participate in making them. It is all very much like a person's handwriting in that each person's designs will be distinctive.

Figure 76 is another example of a junior high school pupil's work. Here, the pupil added interest to his design by cutting into the silhouette and varying the position of the design as he printed each row of his over-all pattern.

Figure 77 is a variation of Figure 76. In this over-all design, the pupil did not follow any set pattern but seemed to print at random. The pattern was made more interesting by varying the value, or lightness and darkness, of the print so that a certain amount of rhythm was achieved in the design.

Figure 78 is another experiment made at the junior high school level. In this experiment the pupil took a piece of foam rubber, dipped it into two different colors, applied it to the colored construction paper, and gave the piece of foam rubber a complete twist while pressing it to the paper.

Figure 79 is an example of another subject area which the children used in their designs. The first design is a simple gray silhouette of a mask against a white background. In this design the object is a dominant part while the background is subordinate. As in any good design, some one thing has to be more important than another. If every part of the design were of equal importance, there would be a tendency toward monotony. By making one thing a little more important, there is variety in the design.

The second design in Figure 79 is a repetition of the first. This time, however, the mask is white and the background is gray. Although the mask shapes are the same, the white one appears to be larger. This is an optical illusion as white and light colors have a tendency to make things appear larger, while black and dark colors make things appear smaller.

The third design in Figure 79 is another repetition of the first design. It is a little more interesting because the inside of the mask has been cut out.

The fourth design in Figure 79 is the same as the third, but reverse in value, the object being white and the background gray. It can be noted that the cutout portion of the mask is gray.

The fifth and final design in Figure 79 is made interesting by the combination of the different variations used in all the other designs, plus dividing the design in half and altering its value pattern.

Children at all grade levels like to see their work exhibited. It is a good idea for the teacher and pupils to plan a display at the end of each completed lesson. This means that the pupils' work will have to be evaluated. There are many ways of evaluating the pupils' work. One is in terms of exhibiting the best work from the entire class.

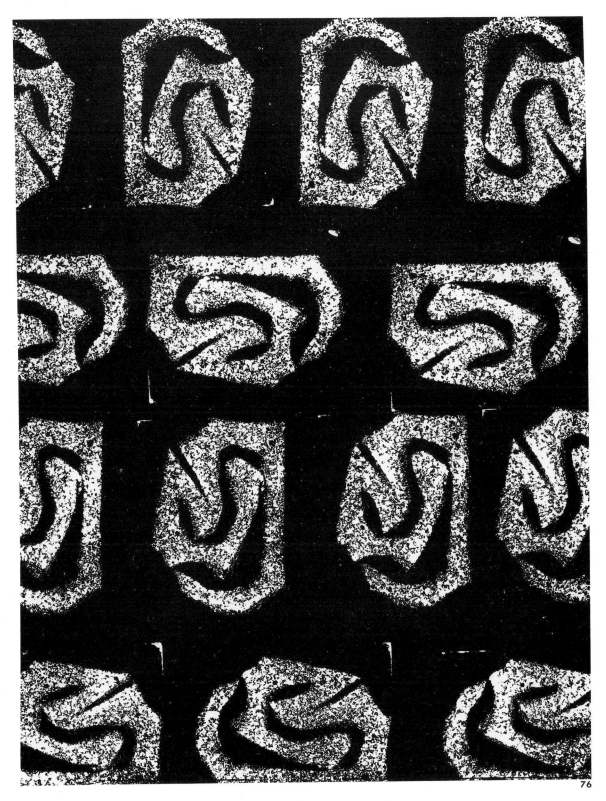

Another way is to exhibit the work of the pupils who showed the most improvement. A display may also be planned to serve as a teaching aid or silent teacher. Whatever the purpose of the display may be, its aims and purposes must be discussed with the pupils and their work evaluated in the light of their objectives.

Figure 80 is an example of a display planned by a committee of three students at the junior high school level. The display was planned as a teaching aid, and the designs were evaluated and selected to show a variety of techniques developed through printing with foam rubber.

There are many uses for things printed with foam rubber such as textile designs, post cards, place cards, wallpaper, shower curtains, and many more.

To summarize the experiments of printing with foam rubber, we learned that materials adapt themselves differently in the way they can be used most effectively. It is only through experimentation that we can become acquainted with the material and use it to its best advantage.

We discovered that not only through working with the material can we understand design, but also through observation of things in nature and man-made objects.

We also learned something about making our designs more interesting by taking into consideration the dominant and subordinate parts of the design. Cutting into a silhouette sometimes adds interest to the design. An over-all pattern which was printed at random can be just as interesting as one that is carefully laid out.

There are many subjects which can be chosen when designing, and in many cases, there are a great many variations within each subject area. This seems to give evidence that there is no limit or end to the amount of design that may be created.

Displays are important and serve many purposes. The aims and objectives of the display, as planned by a committee, may serve as a criteria for evaluating and selecting pupils' work.

Through our observations of pupils at work, here are some words of caution for teachers to help make their teaching more effective and to

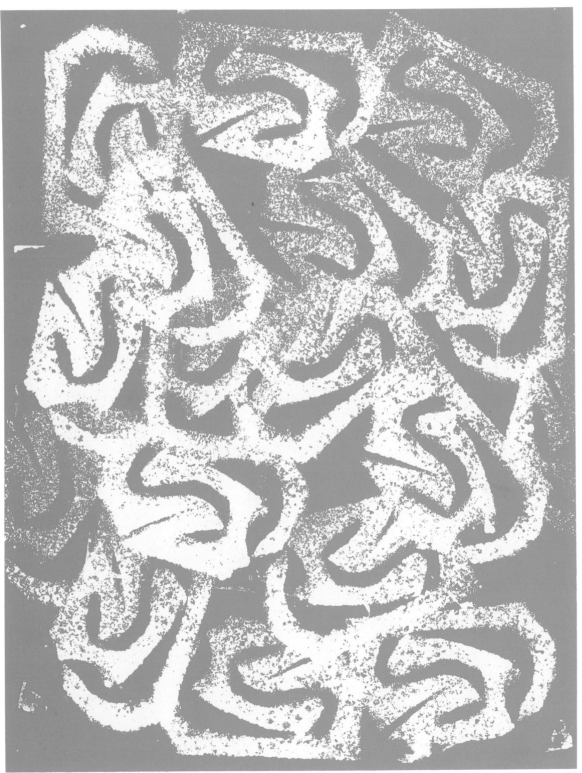

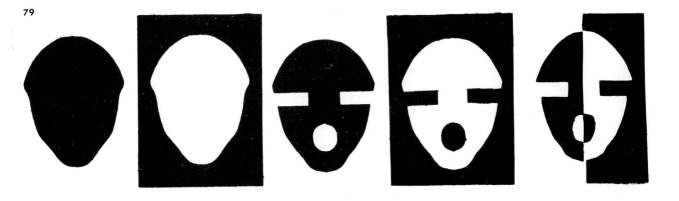

80

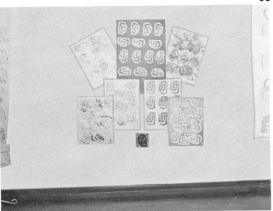

help sustain the interest of children. Teachers should try to keep their lessons "fresh" by not running a project down until the pupils get bored with it. It is surprising how many prints pupils can make in a 45-minute period if the class is conducted properly.

Demonstrations should be clear, brief, and well-planned, to avoid too much talking or lecturing. The emphasis should be placed on learning by doing.

Materials and ample work space should be provided and planned so that the pupil can get the necessary supplies when he needs them.

Teachers should make a study of how much time to allow for presentation, passing material, supervision of the activities, individual instruction, storing of equipment, cleaning up the room, and preparing the class for dismissal. Often an otherwise excellent teaching and learning situation is marred because somewhere along the line the timing was off.

CHAPTER 8

Designs Created With Sink Stoppers, Hoses, and Other Related Materials

Engaging designs can be made with sink stoppers and other materials found in the home. A good feature about some of these materials is that they are already made, and it only remains for the pupils to use their imaginations and discover effective ways of producing attractive designs. Upon examining a sink stopper the students soon found out that it may be adapted for printing admirably well. It even has a handle which is helpful when printing.

Among other things, we observed and learned how interesting space arrangements were made by using circular rubber objects to print with. The experiments were made to suggest three-dimen-

sional objects, movement, and rhythm. These were accomplished by moving the object when printing.

Figures 81 and 82 show some of the materials and tools which were used for printing. Besides sink stoppers, these tools include a rubber doorstop, a pair of rubbers, a piece of hose mounted on a pencil, pencil erasers, assorted washers, a rubber shower head, stamp pad, colored ink, and such papers as tracing paper, colored construction paper, white drawing paper, paper hand toweling, and one-inch squared paper.

Although the circle is not the most interesting shape, 7th grade pupils discovered that a design may be made more pleasing by using two or more

RUBBER HOSE

82

different-sized circles to make for variety in space arrangement, as shown in Figure 83. Interesting space design is accomplished by varying the size of the circles in such a way that the distances between them are not the same. Interest may also be increased by having some of the circles wider than others. Sink stoppers adapt themselves to this principle of design because they come in a number of different sizes. Where even smaller circles were needed, different-sized hoses were used or sometimes washers were used successfully.

All of these objects were substantial enough so that they were used without any backing or re-enforcement. They were also easy to clean and store. Printing with these objects was done in several ways. Ink was applied to the object by using a stamp pad, a roller, or a brush.

Interesting border and surface designs were made by overlapping the circles, thus producing other designs and patterns. Figure 84 is an example of this. When making this design the pupil used a 1 1/8 -inch sink stopper, as well as a stamp pad and paper hand toweling. The circles were printed one next to the other, using a ruler as a guide. When the first line was printed, the ruler was placed the width of the sink stopper, or 9/16 inch below the first line. The circles in the second line were printed over the circles in the first line in such a way that they overlapped the first row half-way at the point where the circles in the first line touched. This method of printing was repeated until the surface pattern was completed. It was noted that by overlapping the circles, other forms were developed which added interest to the surface pattern.

Large surface patterns originally began as simple border designs, using one or more sink stoppers. Later, as one row of a border design was completed below another, they were linked together with smaller circles made with a sink stopper, pencil eraser, and the end of a piece of hose. To get more variety, the smaller solid and open circles were printed off-center. Figure 85 shows the finished product.

Reference has been made to open circles and solid circles in relation to border designs and surface patterns. It is important to point out that designs may be worked out by using good lines, but it is also necessary to understand good light and dark schemes since they give life to line, draw the eye to important parts of the pattern, and make for dominance and subordination in harmonious arrangements.

Figure 86 shows four examples of the use of light and dark. Example A does not have as much contrast with the background as Examples B, C, and D; hence, it does not draw attention to it as much. It is subtle and quieting whereas Example C is dominant and forceful. Example B is the middle value between these two extremities. The gray value between white and black may have an infinite number of steps. These values between the middle value and black are referred to as shades, while those between the middle value and white

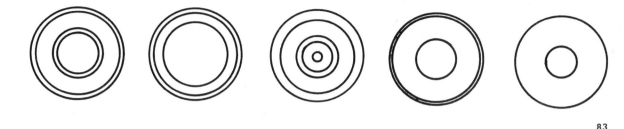

83

84

are called tints. Just as good proportion is observed in line drawing, it is of equal importance to think of it in terms of dark and light elements. Example D in Figure 86 shows the reverse of Example C; here the background is black and the circle is white. As previously mentioned, white areas seem to appear larger than black ones. If the white circle appears larger, it is because of an optical illusion.

Fascinating experiments were made with a rubber shower head by one of the high school pupils, as shown in Figure 87. Figure 88a is a print made with this object after the shower head was rubbed over a piece of sandpaper. The ink was applied with a watercolor brush. The result was not too exciting. By moving the shower head a little while the impression was being made, a much more interesting result was obtained, as shown in Figure 88b.

Whereas the design in Figure 88a is static, the one shown in Figure 88b is vibrant. Figure 88c is a composition made of several designs shown in Figure 88b. The designs seem to be whirling away from the paper, giving the whole pattern a feeling of movement and a three-dimensional effect. The three-dimensional effect is created by the gradation of lines from light to dark, as well as the direction given by the lines.

Figure 88d is an interesting effect achieved by twisting the shower head first to the right a little and then to the left. The movement in this design seems to be in both directions.

Figure 88e was done by giving the shower head an almost complete twist in one direction. The background pattern is almost as interesting as the printed pattern. The lines seem to radiate in a sweeping movement from an imaginary center line.

Figure 88f was made by dragging the shower head in one direction while making the impression. The result gives the viewer a feeling of speed such as is related to a rocket ship that surges with power.

The unusual pattern shown in Figure 88g was accomplished by moving the shower head in the direction of a figure eight while making the impression. Upon closer observation, it will be noted that the direction of the lines seems to give the design a depth, or a third-dimensional effect. It suggests a twisted tube made of wires that starts at nowhere and fades out into space or infinity.

These experiments seem to point out that from a comparatively uninteresting impression made with a rubber shower head, exciting designs can be created if a little imagination is applied.

A surprisingly elegant surface pattern was created by a high school pupil using a rubber doorstop and a pair of rubbers—two common and unexciting objects. Figure 89 shows the result obtained. In this surface pattern the sole of the rubber boot was pressed into yellow water-soluble ink which had been spread and rolled out with a roller on a piece of 9 by 12 inch glass. The impressions were made on a sheet of 18 by 24 inch black mounting paper. It is a drop repeat surface pattern. The rubber doorstop was pressed into red ink. Interest was added by overlapping the doorstop impressions with each other and also overlapping the doorstop impressions with those made by the sole of the rubber boot. Contrast in

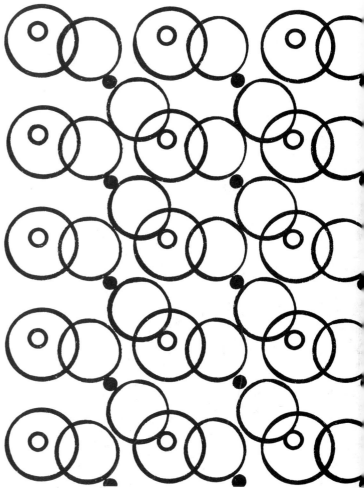

85

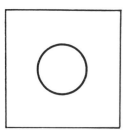

A

B

C

D

86

88a

88b

88c

88d

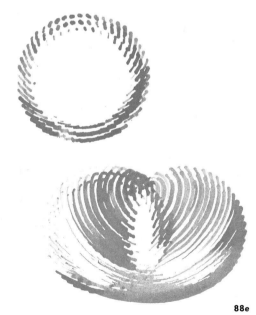

88e

value of the colors and background and the texture and shape of the rubber sole and doorstop all helped to make the design a fascinating one.

Figure 90 is a surface pattern created by a 1st grade student. A small rubber ball was dipped into tempera colors and the print was made. The design is carried out in red-violet and blue.

Figure 91 was made by a 2nd grade student.

88f

88g

In this experiment the child used broken rubber bands which were dipped into tempera paint; red and blue colors were used. The dots were made by the paint which dropped when the rubber bands were placed and removed from the paper. Tempera colors are used a great deal for printing in the lower grades because they are inexpensive to use and easy to clean up.

A piece of rubber tubing was cut and glued on a piece of cardboard by a 3rd grade student to make the over-all design shown in Figure 92. Blue tempera color was brushed on the design and the impressions made. The openings within the design add interest.

An interesting variety of shapes was achieved by using a combination of impressions made with canning jar rubbers, as shown in Figure 93. This design was made by a 5th grade pupil.

Pupils in practically all grades can experiment with common rubber household objects. Some have decorated school bags and book covers with rubber objects; others have made border designs which were used for shelf-edging. Many designs could be used for window curtains, rug and carpet designs, and textiles of all kinds.

89

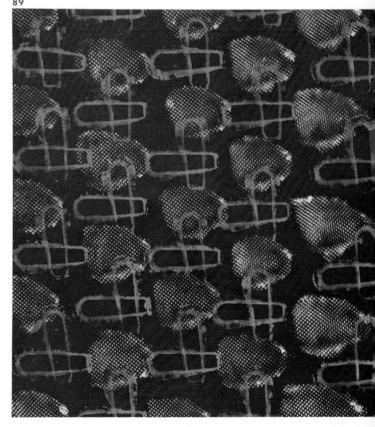

90

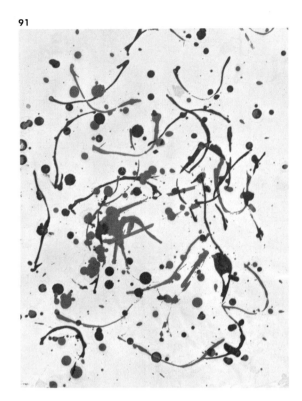

91

92

In evaluating pupils' work, emphasis was placed on new and exciting ways of creating designs. Pupils explored a great many and variety of rubber objects with which to print. Looking for objects to print with helps to develop the power of observation and ability to visualize what could be accomplished with the objects. The work was also evaluated in terms of the discoveries pupils made about design which would help them grow and develop. In some classes pupils kept a folder of all the experiments they made from the beginning to the end of the project. These folders proved valuable for there was a step-by-step record which gave concrete evidence of the progress or lack of progress made by the pupil.

93

In summarizing the findings of the experiments shown and discussed in this chapter, it may be said that a great many rubber objects may be found around the home which can be used to print new and exciting designs. We learned that although the circle is a rather uninteresting form, we can print exciting designs by overlapping and creating new and more interesting forms. Interest may be added by varying the size and thickness of the circles and by having solid and open circles.

Movement and three-dimensional effects may be accomplished by twisting the object when the impression is made. Three-dimensional effect is obtained by the direction of the line and gradation of the value of the color used. Three-dimensional is synonomous with depth.

Objects of contrasting shapes and textures, as well as contrasting colors, add interest to the designs.

Printing with rubber objects can be an exciting adventure at all grade levels.

Many teachers agree that the use of tempera color is probably the least expensive way of printing. It is also easier to clean up

94

CHAPTER 9

Designs Created With Assorted Objects and Materials

This chapter has to do with pupils' experiments in printing conducted with many different kinds of objects and materials at different grade levels. Some of the objects and materials used included the following: corrugated paper, string, buttons, wood, evergreen leaves, stones, toy wheels, razor blades, bow ties, and a scrub brush.

In addition to these materials and objects, the following supplies were used: a roll of paper hand toweling, construction paper of different colors, unprinted newspaper sheets, large sheets of manila paper, mounting paper, inks, rollers, brushes, scissors, knives, tempera colors, paper used for padding to facilitate printing, clean rags, and other common materials and tools which are usually available in an art room.

Figure 94 shows two students in junior high school printing designs with corrugated paper on long strips of paper hand toweling. These pupils used a portable bulletin board which was covered with green burlap. This made an excellent cushion when printing. Other pupils used several large manila sheets or newspapers.

It was found best to make large, bold designs when working with corrugated paper since any detail was lost in the printing.

A pair of ordinary pointed scissors were used and the designing was done directly with the

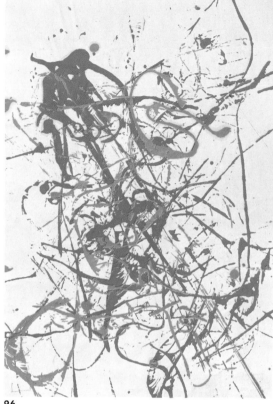
95

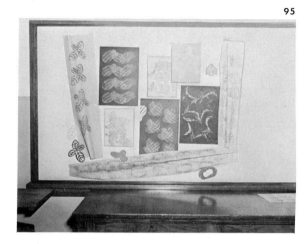

96

scissors while cutting. Tempera color was rolled on with a roller as shown in Figure 94.

Figure 95 shows a bulletin board arranged with some of the results obtained by the students. With some of the over-all surface designs are shown the cutout corrugated designs which were used to make the patterns.

Some pupils felt that the designs printed with corrugated paper appeared as if they were vibrating; others mentioned that they were reminded of window curtain designs. Interesting cross-hatch effects were made by overlapping designs when printing. Some over-all patterns were done in several colors. Because corrugated paper is fairly stiff, it required no other material to re-enforce it. Regular corrugated cardboard boxes obtained from grocery stores were used.

First grade pupils conducted fascinating experiments by printing with string. Figure 96 shows an exciting design made by dropping a piece of string on the paper after it had been dipped in

tempera paint. It was then lifted, dipped in paint, and dropped again on the paper. This was repeated until the desired effect was achieved. Strings of different ply were used with different colors.

In Figure 97 another pupil used the same technique on half of the paper. The sheet was then folded over and an impression made on the other half.

Figure 98 is an example of still another technique developed by one the students. In this example, the student dropped the string and gently pulled it over the paper. Still another pupil dropped the string on one side, folded the paper and pulled the string out. The result is shown in Figure 99.

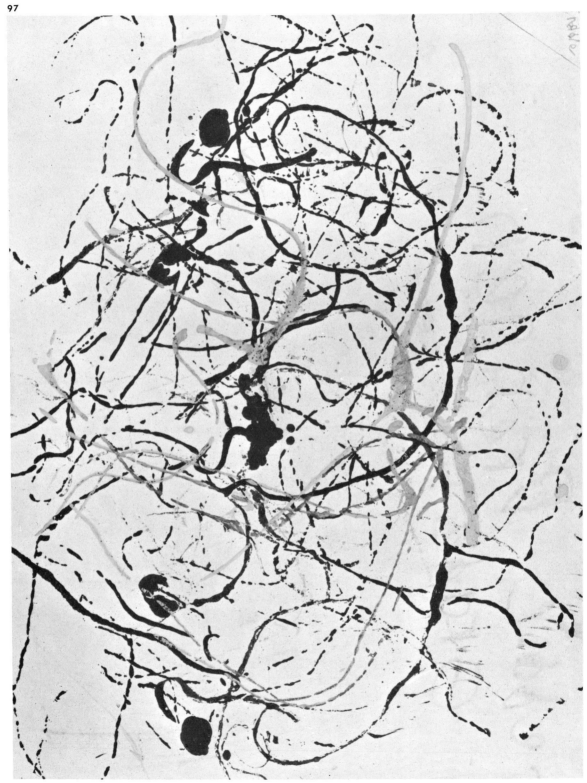

98

99

Figures 100 and 101 are designs made by students using a combination of the above-mentioned techniques. Many of these designs have a great deal of movement to them and appear to be enlarged microscopic prints of bacteria in action. Still others seem to resemble muscle tissues and cells.

Although no example was available, one of the pupils experimented with designs by squeezing Duco cement on a cardboard with the intention of later making impressions by applying paint after the cement was dry on the cardboard.

Figure 102 is another example of a unique surface pattern made by an elementary grade student. This random pattern was printed with a button. The lighter impressions seem to fade into the background while the darker ones seem to advance. This gives the pattern depth. A brush was used to apply black tempera color to the button.

Figure 103 shows several simple border designs printed by a junior high school student with different kinds of buttons which he found in his mother's sewing box. The buttons were pressed onto an ink pad which was impregnated with India ink.

101

Old, weatherbeaten pieces of wood were used by 5th grade pupils to produce the results shown in Figures 104 and 105. Tempera colors were brushed over the pieces of wood which were then pressed against the paper. The design in Figure 104 was printed with red and black, while the one in Figure 105 was done with orange and blue. In both designs one color was superimposed over the other. These two prints, where the same material was used, are shown to point out the difference in texture of different pieces of wood. Unusual prints were made by using the end grain of different kinds of wood as well as bark and small branches.

A rather delicate pattern was created by printing with a piece of evergreen as shown in Figure 106. It was made by a high school pupil. India ink was poured into an aluminum pie pan, and the one side of a piece of evergreen was dipped into it. The evergreen was then placed on colored construction paper, a sheet of paper was placed over the evergreen, and gentle pressure was applied.

Another 5th grade pupil brought stones of various sizes, brushed on the paint, and printed the design shown in Figure 107. Three colors were used. Some children dipped the stones into tempera colors and rolled them over the paper. Figure 108 represents the results of an ingenious technique. A small toy car was rolled over tempera color, which had been spread on a piece of glass, and then was rolled on the paper. These are the wheel tracks.

Figures 109, 110, and 111 are over-all prints done by a pupil at the junior high school level. Tempera color was applied to the razor blade with a brush and printed as shown in Figure 109. The bow tie and hand scrub brush were dipped into the tempera color and printed to produce the effects shown in Figures 110 and 111. When using the hand scrub brush, some pupils obtained a variety of interesting results by applying different pressure to the brush when printing. Others twisted the brush when making the print.

Many of the surface patterns created by making impressions with assorted objects and materials can have application in everyday life as well as in industry. For example, they can be used

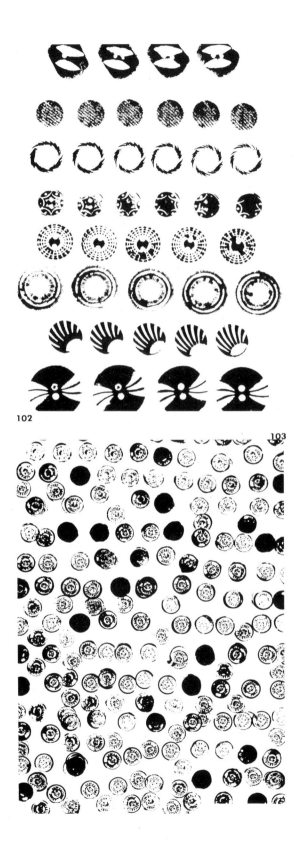

102

103

to design curtains, floor covering, wallpaper, wrapping paper, and in textile designs for sport shirts and dresses.

When evaluating the work presented in this chapter, we were concerned with how well we explored the variety of assorted objects and materials. We were interested to see how these objects look when printed as objects in themselves and how we could make prints that had an interesting and harmonious arrangement of line, mass, or color or a combination of two or all three of these elements.

Certain objects or materials were selected because they had beautiful lines, textures or colors, an unusual shape, or because they behaved in ways that could be used to make interesting designs. Some objects were chosen because they furnished a motif for a design.

In summarizing, we may say that we had only begun to explore the many objects that could be utilized for printing. We found it to be an exciting and intriguing experience. We discovered inter-

105

106

esting techniques and combinations of techniques with which to create designs with good arrangement. We found that we could plan good compositions, as well as achieve them by working freely and in a random way. We learned that surface

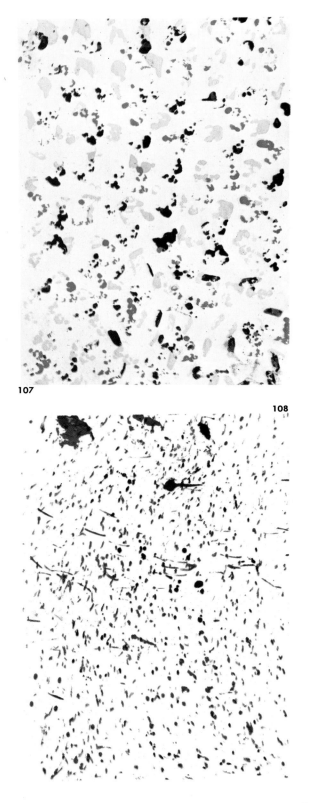

107

108

patterns may appear to be delicate, bold, vibrant, squirming, three-dimensional, crisp, rhythmic, exciting, clean, restful, forceful, and possess many other qualities. They may remind us of other things such as microbes, muscles, and many other objects.

110

We learned that through the gathering of material and experimentation we collect a great deal of facts and information so that with this knowledge we may express ourselves better. We also discovered many different techniques to help us create designs.

Teachers are cautioned not to make the collecting of objects or the learning of a variety of techniques ends in themselves or "busy work."

109

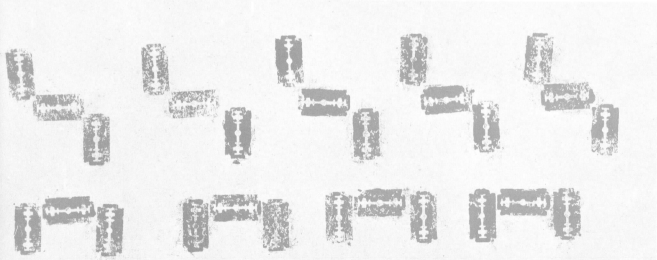

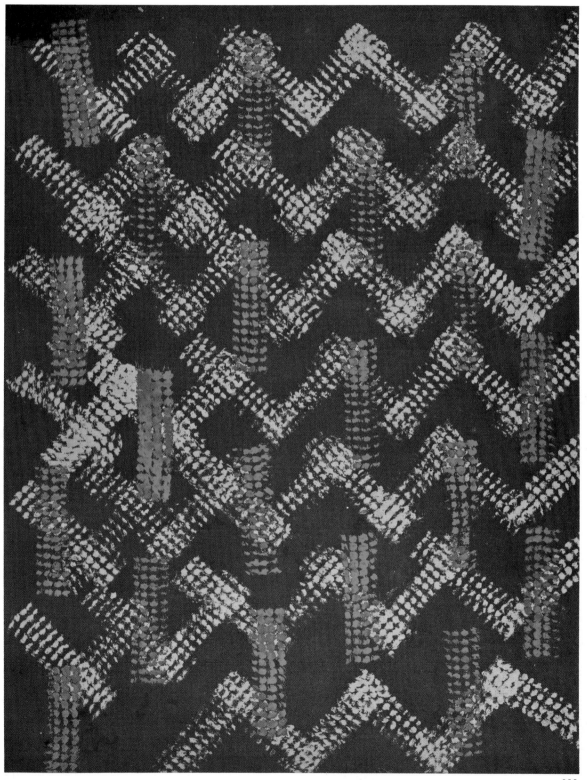

CHAPTER 10

Designs Created With a Variety of Erasers and Other Office Supplies

Almost every home, office, and school has a large assortment of pencil and ink erasers, as well as other objects which can be used to print interesting and unusual designs. The students found that these objects offered almost unlimited opportunities for them to do creative printing and learn something about the principles and elements of design. Pupils were encouraged to experiment, to discover, and to explore new and different ways of exploiting the materials and objects.

Some of the objects and materials used in the projects which are included in this chapter were corrugated paper, rubber bands, rubber cement, a small window squeegee, an assortment of large

pencil and ink erasers, a penknife, V-shaped and U-shaped linoleum cutting tools, India ink, printer's ink, stamp pads, different kinds of paper, a roller, a 9 by 12 inch piece of glass, sandpaper, and other common tools and materials found in the art room.

After assembling some of these objects and materials, the pupils were ready to start this exciting adventure. The pupils in the elementary grades decided to experiment with rubber bands, a small squeegee, and a secretary's typewriter eraser. Figure 112 shows a student experimenting with some of these objects.

Rubber bands fascinated the children because

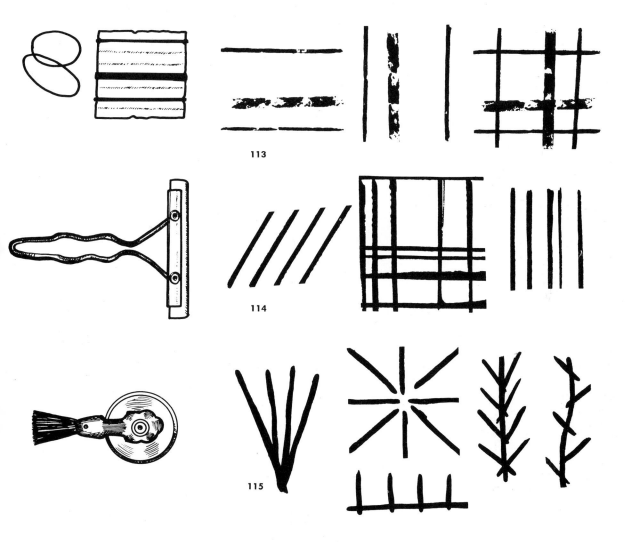

113

114

115

they come in many sizes, widths, thicknesses, and colors. To hold the rubber bands in place the children cut a piece of corrugated paper to the desired size. In order to prevent the erasers from slipping off the corrugated paper, a square or rectangle was cut to a size the length of the erasers and notched as shown in Figure 113.

An interesting plaid design was created by an elementary pupil. Since rubber bands come in many widths, this helped to add variety to the plaid. The same rubber band stamp was first used in a horizontal position; then it was superimposed vertically on the horizontal print. Ink was applied to the rubber bands with a small watercolor brush.

An inked stamp pad was also used. Figure 121 shows how this design was carried out as a surface pattern. It can be noticed that an unusual textural effect is produced by the rubber bands.

Figure 114 shows a familiar household object, a small window squeegee. Ink was applied to the squeegee by pressing it directly on an inked glass plate or by using a small watercolor brush. Pupils practiced printing diagonal, horizontal, and vertical lines or a combination of lines to produce different kinds of designs. Since the thickness of the lines is the same, particular attention was given to good space division which is something that will be discussed later on in this chapter.

A secretary's typewriter eraser as shown in Figure 115 brought no end of fascination to the youngsters because printing is accomplished by rolling rather than pressing. Ink was applied to the circular eraser by rolling it over block printing ink which was spread out with a roller over a piece of glass or a tin plate. A circular eraser that revolves like a wheel on an axle is an absorbing and exciting tool which stimulates the imagination and may be used as a motivating force to encourage students to do creative work. Straight, curved, and wavy lines may be made with this eraser. This tool proved to be a successful means to get young people acquainted with the principle of radiation. The examples shown illustrate this principle of radiation. The first is an example of radiation from a base point. The second is radiation from the center of a circle as seen in flower and other naturalistic or man-made objects and below that is radiation from a base line. Next, is radiation from a straight line and finally, radiation from a curved line.

Since the materials and objects previously mentioned give the students a great deal of opportunity to experiment with space divisions, the work of Piet Mondrian has been included in Figure 116 to show how one artist used interesting space divisions most effectively. Mondrian used horizontal and vertical lines when he expressed himself. The emphasis is on the right angle which gives his work directness, simplicity, and a feeling of formality.

Horizontal lines suggest breadth, placidity, or restfulness. Vertical lines are also restful and suggest aspiration and height. Perhaps these ideas or thoughts were in Mondrian's mind when he expressed himself through painting about the world in which he lived.

Horizontal and vertical lines are shown in Figure 117a and b, together with other lines which suggest different feelings. Some lines may suggest an upward sweeping movement, as shown in Figure 117c. This movement may suggest fire. Figure 117d gives the feeling of compression, squeezing, or forcing together, while Figure 117e produces the reverse effect of expanding, enlarging, or giving more breathing space. Figure 117f is radiation from a point and suggests the explosion produced by a bomb, an exertion of force outward from the center. It may also suggest the sun. Lines may also suggest slow, fast, gradual, graceful, consistent, and other kinds of movement. They may also suggest a squirming motion as shown in Figure 117g. Jagged, irregular lines as shown in Figure 117h suggest agitation, while lines as shown in Figure 117i suggest slow motion without a sense of direction as, for example, the movement of a fish in a bowl or bacteria under a microscope.

By looking at Figure 118a, it can be readily seen that lines drawn at regular intervals appear to be monotonous because of the sameness. By examining Figure 118b, we note that it seems more interesting because the distances between the lines are different. In Figure 118c the thickness of the lines was varied and the spaces between

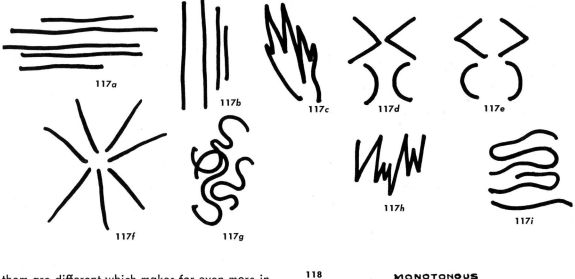

117a

117b

117c

117d

117e

117f

117g

117h

117i

them are different which makes for even more interest. By looking at Mondrian's painting, we can see how skillfully he used this principle.

Figure 119a shows an uninteresting horizontal and vertical division of a rectangle. Since the resulting four smaller rectangles are the same, there is no choice. Figures 119b and 119c show good divisions. Figure 119b illustrates a more dramatic effect while Figure 119c is more subtle. It seems that by dividing a shape off-center, more interest is created. If we observe Mondrian's painting

118

MONOTONOUS

VARIED & INTERESTING

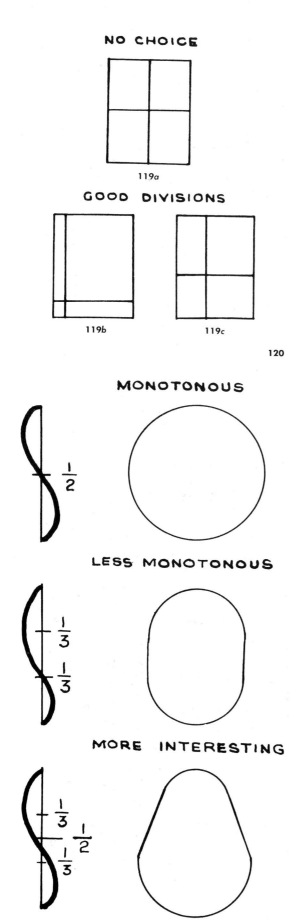

NO CHOICE

119a

GOOD DIVISIONS

119b   119c

120

MONOTONOUS

$\frac{1}{2}$

LESS MONOTONOUS

$\frac{1}{3}$

$\frac{1}{3}$

MORE INTERESTING

$\frac{1}{3}$ $\frac{1}{2}$

$\frac{1}{3}$

again, we find that he applied this principle almost consistently throughout the painting. Some of the space divisions through which he expressed himself were dramatic, others more subtle. Perhaps this was the way he saw the world in which he lived.

Figure 120 pointed out to the pupils that interesting space divisions may be observed in many shapes, and by dividing a shape off-center, more variety and interest was produced.

Both the vertical and horizontal lines may be moved about anywhere to produce designs with interesting proportions. It is difficult to say whether the subtle variations or the dramatic ones are better, for this depends on personal preference and has to do in a large measure with the temperament of the individual who is making the choice. The important thing to remember is that the individual has a choice or selection to make. Here we see how individual differences and preferences come into play, rather than the idea of what is "good design."

Pupils in the upper elementary grades and junior high school discovered that with a few ordinary tools and large soap erasers, approximately 1 by 1 by 1 ½ inches in size, interesting and unusual designs could be created. The possibilities seemed limitless.

Figure 122 shows a pupil busily engaged in printing with an eraser. In the background are some of the materials and tools used for this project, including linoleum cutting tools, the erasers, paper, and an ink pad.

Erasers are fun to work with; they are soft, pliable, easily cut, clean, a good size to work with, and need no reenforcing. Six sides of the eraser may be used to print with.

When designing eraser stamps, pupils discovered that there were several ways to produce them. They found out that designs could be made by cutting into the eraser with a veiner or V-shaped linoleum cutting tool, thus making an incised or intaglio design. Another way was to transfer the design to the eraser and cut away the background. This left the design raised and made it a relief design. Some designs which were created were both relief and intaglio. Many pupils used the flat, broad side of the eraser to print the background color; actually they were employing the planographic type of printing.

Figure 123 is an example of a surface design made by a pupil in junior high school. This surface pattern was an elaboration of a simple border design. First, the pupil experimented by repeating the unit several times; then he reversed the position of the design as he printed. In the final surface design, it can be noticed that the unit was printed right side up, then the design was turned upside down and overlapped when printed. There are almost countless variations that can be done with a unit of design. Interesting and different arrangements result from experimentation. In the lower right-hand portion of Figure 123 is an enlargement of the design unit. This unit is a simplification of a design of a tree. Part of the design was carved out in relief and part was incised. The end of a 1 by 1 by 1½ inch soap eraser was

used. The design was first cut out of paper and then traced on the eraser with a wax pencil. When working with the linoleum cutting tools, the veiner, or V-shaped tool, was used for outlining the design. The incised parts of the design were also done with the veiner. The U-shaped tool, called a gouge, was used to remove wider areas of the eraser, such as the background of the design. A penknife was used to sharpen up the detailed part of the design. The design was not cut too deep, about an eighth of an inch sufficed. What was more important was that the depth had to be uniform. If the background of the design was not cut out evenly, raised irregularities registered during printing. Stamp pads were used very successfully for printing the designs which were carved in soap erasers.

Pupils experimented by printing on a scrap piece of paper before carrying out any project.

121

When the print was not uniform after several tries, it was because the surface of the eraser was not straight and level. In that case, the eraser was placed on a sheet of fine sandpaper and gently rubbed up and down a few times and then from side to side.

Figure 124 is a simple floral relief design with a white background made by a junior high school pupil. It is a drop design which simply means that the design units are not all in a straight line, but every other one is dropped. By alternating the units, the surface pattern is made a little more interesting.

Figure 125 is an incised bird design. It too is a drop design, and in this case the second unit was dropped about two-thirds the distance of the first unit.

Figure 126 is an example of a design made by a junior high school pupil using the planographic and relief type of printing. In this surface pattern the background was printed with the broad, flat part of an eraser after yellow ink had been applied to the eraser with a brush. The pupil varied the background pattern and the relief design which he superimposed on the background color to add interest.

122

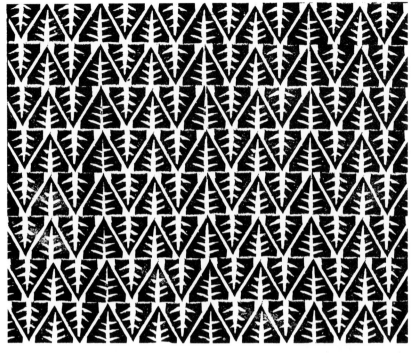

123

124

When creating designs which could be used for eraser printing, the pupils used a round-nib pen because the curved lines made with this kind of a pen approximated the curved lines that were made with a linoleum cutting tool.

Figure 127 shows a selection of a variety of subjects used for designs. These designs by pupils in the upper elementary and junior high school grades were made with a round-nib pen.

The experiment in Figure 128 shows how variety in design can be produced by placing the dominant part of the design in a different position in relation to the subordinate part. When repeated, each one of these variations would bring about a different over-all effect.

Pupils in the upper elementary grades and junior high school also experimented with an assortment of erasers of different sizes, shapes,

125

82

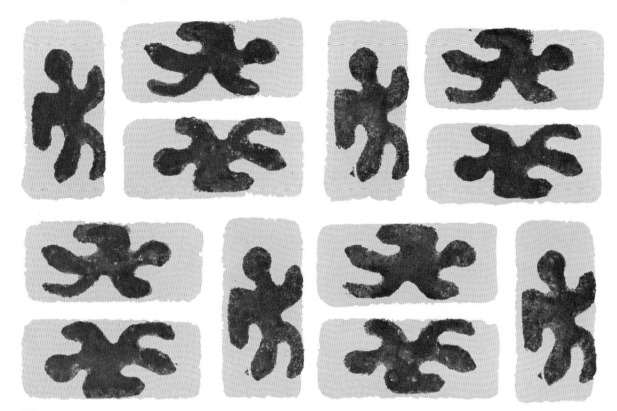

126

127

128

129

and colors. In this project the object was to discover the many possibilities that the shape and size of an eraser could suggest when creating designs. For example, a long, thin eraser could be curved and bent.

Figure 129 shows a junior high school pupil busily at work cutting a design into the edge of an eraser. Some of the materials and tools used in this project are also shown. In addition to the tools shown in Figure 129, pupils used colored inks, brushes, and all kinds of white and colored drawing paper.

Figure 130a shows an interesting experiment done by cutting into the edge of an eraser and bending it while printing. Pupils used rubber bands and string to retain the bend in the eraser. Figure 130b shows another experiment done with the same bent eraser. The student varied the position of the eraser when printing in such a way that the curved parts of the design fitted into one another. A surface pattern was created that seems to have a feeling of movement throughout it.

Although there are many shapes, children were not exposed to the many different kinds of forms which would increase their scope of designing. At first they became acquainted with a few simple

130a

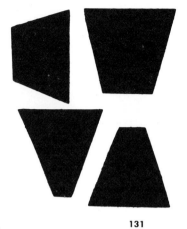

131

132

133

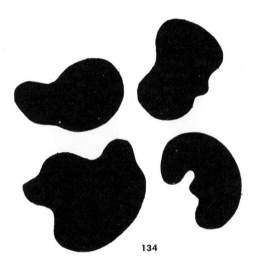

134

135

136

137

geometric shapes, such as a square, rectangle, circle, and triangle.

Figure 131 shows rectangular forms of different sizes that are commonly used for surface designing compiled and cut out by a high school pupil. Figure 132 shows common varieties of triangular shapes, while Figure 133 shows a variety of curvilinear shapes. Figure 134 shows some free forms sometimes referred to as an amoeba shape, a zoological term which means a simple form of animal life consisting of a single cell which moves by finger-like extensions. The illustrated shapes seem to be graphic representations of this description.

Figure 135 shows interesting shapes which are a combination of rectangular shapes and amoeba shapes. These may also be seen in many contemporary designs used for utilitarian purposes. Figure 136 shows exciting, dynamic rectilinear shapes which appear to be more interesting than those shown in Figures 131 and 132 since there is more variation. It also seems as if they are a combination of both the shapes shown in Figures 131 and 132. Figure 137 shows forms worthwhile to explore since they give a feeling of depth. They are also rectilinear shapes which stimulate perspective. There are many more forms which may be discovered and explored.

Figure 138 is a monogram stamp design which was incised in a dynamic rectilinear shape. Monogram designs had to be traced and cut in reverse so that when printed the letters were in their

138

139

140

natural position. The monogram was enriched by using a repeat border in the upper right and lower left of the stamp.

Figure 139 is a surface pattern made by a junior high school pupil. It was incised in a curvilinear shape which suggests a leaf-design motif. Radiation is the design principle used in this motif. To be more specific, it is radiation from a curved line. The shape is the original size and shape of the eraser, sometimes referred to as a pink pearl eraser. This design was developed by making several outlines of the pink pearl eraser on a sheet of drawing paper and then experimenting with different ideas, using a grease pencil. After selecting the most appropriate design, it was transferred on to the pink pearl eraser by placing a sheet of carbon paper against the eraser, putting the design over it, and tracing with a pencil. The design was then cut out with a veiner, and a black stamp pad was used for printing.

This is another example of an incised design. When using a veiner or any other cutting tool, the pupils made sure that the tool was sharp as only a sharp tool will give a clean-cut line. Because erasers are made of a soft material, there is a tendency for people to use dull tools since they feel that the tool will easily cut the material. Dull tools make work more difficult and instead of cutting, they seem to rip into the material and leave a crumbing edge.

Each kind of eraser has a different texture; some erasers are soft and pliable while others, especially the ink erasers, are hard and gritty. Each of these erasers has a different "feel" to it and behaves differently when being cut. It is only through a little experimentation and practice that the students were able to understand better the material with which they were working.

Another interesting project was done by pupils in the junior high school. This project had to do with experimenting and exploring the potentialities of printing with pencil erasers. Rubber erasers at the end of a pencil are a familiar sight. A pencil with an eraser makes a good printing tool because the pencil serves as a convenient holder while the eraser makes an effective stamp.

Figure 140 shows a junior high school pupil

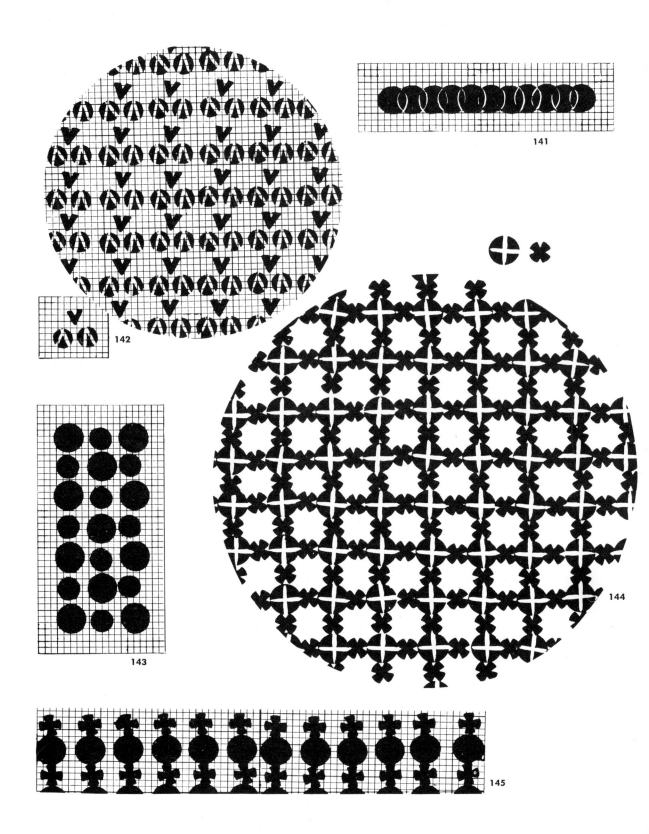

141

142

143

144

145

printing with a pencil eraser. It also shows some of the tools and materials used which included a variety of different textured paper, graph paper, pencils with erasers of different sizes, a stamp pad, a sharp knife, and a single-edge razor blade.

At first pupils made simple experiments to get acquainted with the materials and tools. It was discovered that by gently rubbing the pencil eraser over fine sandpaper while holding it in a perpendicular position, a good flat even surface resulted.

Figure 141 shows a simple border design which was made by printing with the flat even surface of the eraser and overlapping each impression. In this experiment the pupil was practicing to obtain consistently good impressions of uniform value. It can be noticed that where the impressions were overlapped another value was produced. Graph paper was used for this experiment.

Figure 142 shows the use of the same size eraser into which a V-shaped design was cut with a sharp knife. This was an incised design. The same V-shape was cut out of the eraser, and it became a raised or relief design. The incised V appeared the color of the paper with the background black while the relief V appeared black with the background the color of the paper. The circle shows the surface pattern developed using the two pencil stamps.

Figure 143 was a simple practice experiment using two different sized pencil erasers, while Figure 144 shows a simple design cut into the large eraser and another design with the background cut out from the small eraser. The circle shows a pleasant pattern developed by alternating the large and small designs, vertically and horizontally, when printing. The use of these two designs in this way has created another design which seems to grow out of the white background. This design was printed on tissue paper which was placed over graph paper. The graph paper lines were used as a guide to print over.

Figure 145 shows an example of a solid, bold border design. The designs in this experiment were cut with a sharp penknife.

Instead of looking for a certain size of a pencil eraser, different sizes can be made with an eraser that replaces the lead or graphite in a pencil. This eraser is placed in a pencil sharpener and sharpened to a point. It can then be cut along the point to get any desired size.

Figure 146 shows some of the different possibilities of creating unique border designs by using a V-shaped relief design in different positions.

Figure 147 shows several simple geometric shapes which were made with an eraser that was at the end of a pencil. Although the shapes are different, the variation of these shapes was the same. The first variation of the geometric shape was made by reducing and incising its contours inside of the shape. The second variation was an elaboration of the first plus enrichment of the edges which was accomplished by cutting into the sides of the geometric shapes. The third variation was done by cutting from the outside into the eraser and connecting the center part of the design. The design was then divided into four separate but similar units. The fourth variation was done by incising a different geometric shape over the original one. There are many more variations.

Many of the designs created by the pupils had numerous possible uses as surface patterns for objects used in everyday life. Some surface patterns could make attractive wall decorations, textile designs used for draperies, bedspreads, sport shirts, handbags, handkerchiefs, shawls, and other objects made of fabric, as well as for linoleum prints, wallpapers, and tiles.

In evaluating the pupils' work which was used for this chapter, it may be said that pupils in the upper elementary grades through junior high school found printing with erasers a challenging and exciting experience. When experimenting and exploring the possibilities of erasers for

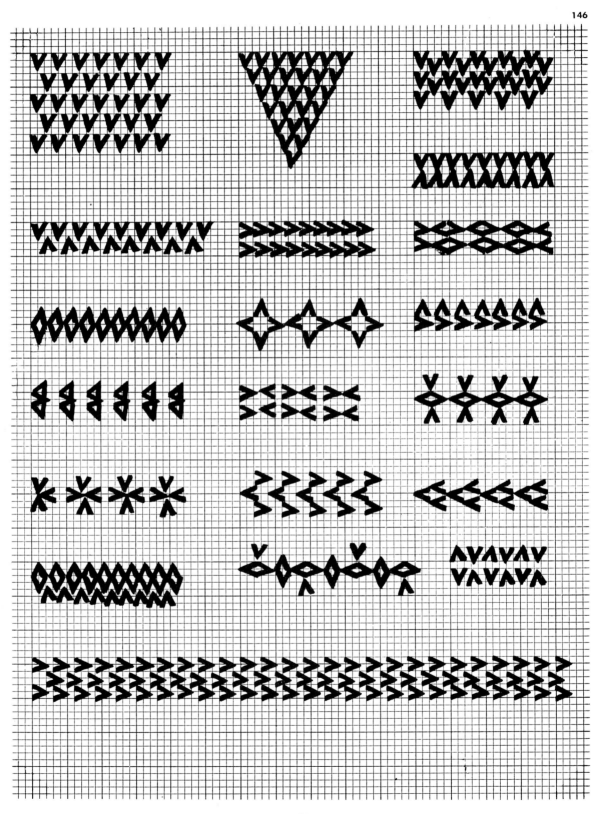

printing, the pupils learned a great deal about design. The use of common everyday objects such as a simple squeegee created a great deal of interest, and children got quick results when printing with it.

Use of a variety of materials to print with not only creates interest but motivates the pupils to discover other objects and techniques through which they can effectively express their ideas and thoughts. Erasers proved to be an excellent material to help pupils carry out their thoughts

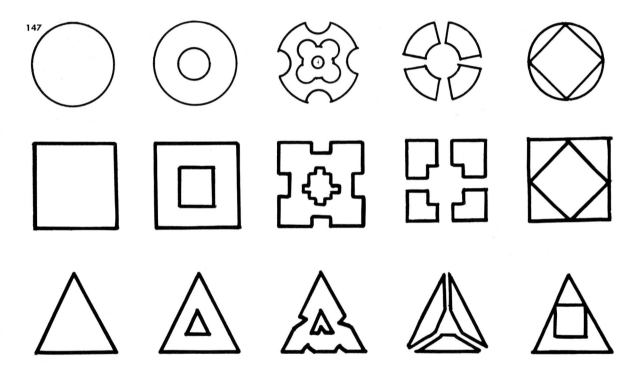

147

and ideas. Printing with erasers also helped to make the pupils work in an organized and orderly manner, to develop good work habits, and to appreciate the work of others.

Teachers should see to it that children learn to use sharp tools with care and caution. It is recommended that sharp tools such as V-shaped or U-shaped gouges should be used only by pupils in the upper elementary grades. It seems that pupils below that level have not acquired the necessary manipulative skills and appreciation of these tools to handle them safely and effectively.

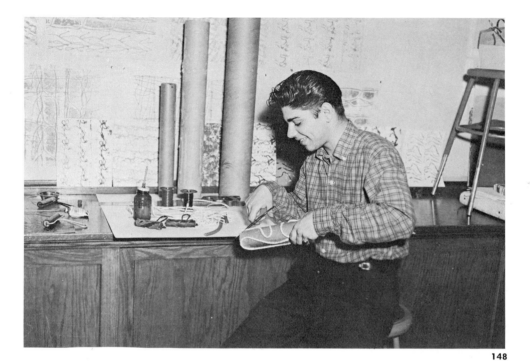

148

CHAPTER 11

Designs Created With a Roller

An impression made by rolling a design over a surface is not a new idea. In the Introduction to this book several exhibits were presented to show different ways of printing, some of them used several thousands of years ago. For example, Figure 1 illustrated the use of a cylinder seal and impression dated 2500-2200 B.C. What was important to many pupils in the class was the fact that to them it was a new discovery and quite accidentally discovered when one of the students found some old paper cylinders which were used as a core to roll paper on. The following experiments are presented to show some of the interesting results obtained.

Some of the experiments included designs printed with rollers of different sizes with a variety of materials in order to encourage pupils to explore and express their own ideas, as well as to understand and appreciate good design.

The materials and tools used for these experiments included the following: large cylindrical tubes (linoleum and rug stores are a good source of supply for these), assortment of string, rope, rubber tubes, upholstery trim material and similar

94

materials, rubber cement, scissors, printers' ink, tempera colors, rubber rollers, a piece of glass 9 by 12 inches, a carpenter's saw for cutting paper tubes, and tin snips for cutting rope and other thick materials.

Figure 148 shows a senior high school boy putting the finishing touches on his roller design. After having selected a large paper roll, he cut a piece approximately a foot long with a carpenter's crosscut saw, applied rubber cement with a brush, and allowed it to dry. Next, he applied rubber cement to a piece of rope approximately four feet long. When the rubber cement dried, he began creating a design over the cylinder by carefully guiding the rope and forming a variety of loops. He worked with or followed the natural tendency of the rope to bend rather than forcing it to curve which is not meant for this material. While shaping the design, he pressed

149

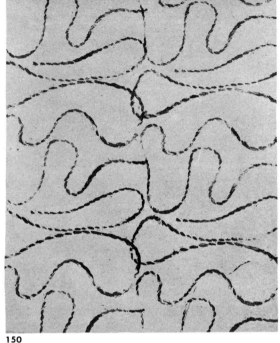

150

the material against the cylinder. When the entire cylinder was gone over, he cut off the surplus rope. He rolled the cylinder over a flat surface, each time a little harder until the rope was securely adhered to the cylinder. Another pupil applied printers' ink to the same roller design by rolling it over a glass plate on which the ink was spread. Figure 149 shows how the ink is applied to the roller. Figure 150 is an example of the result obtained.

Figure 151 is an experiment conducted by using an ordinary rubber roller, applying printers' ink to it, then rolling the roller over a piece of string. The ink on the roller was sufficient to hold the string in place. The roller was then rolled over the ink again and finally an impression was made on the paper.

Different effects can be produced by applying greater or lesser amounts of ink to the roller and varying the pressure while printing. Figure 152a is an experiment showing a line design and a combination line and mass design. The line design was printed by applying a smaller amount of ink

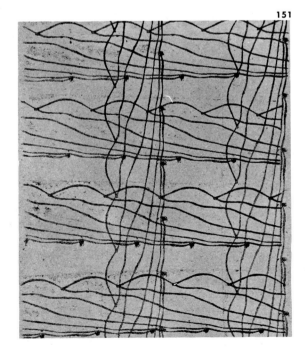

151

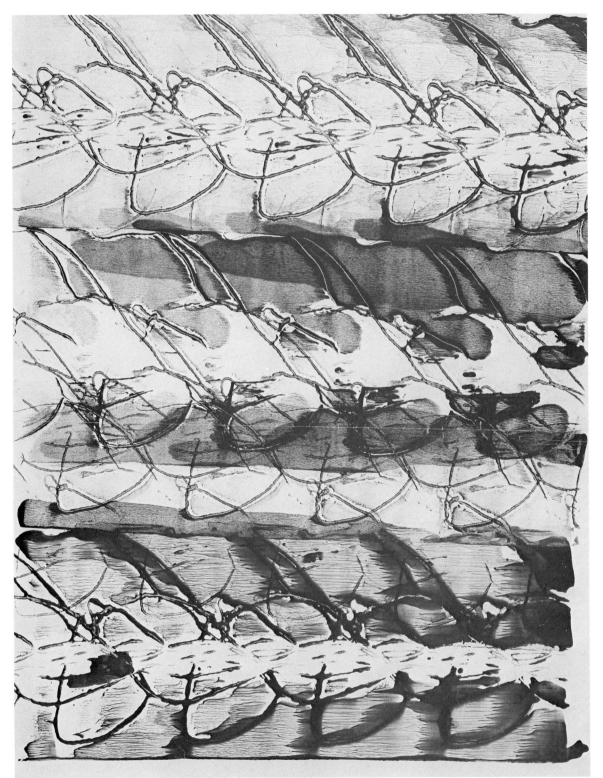

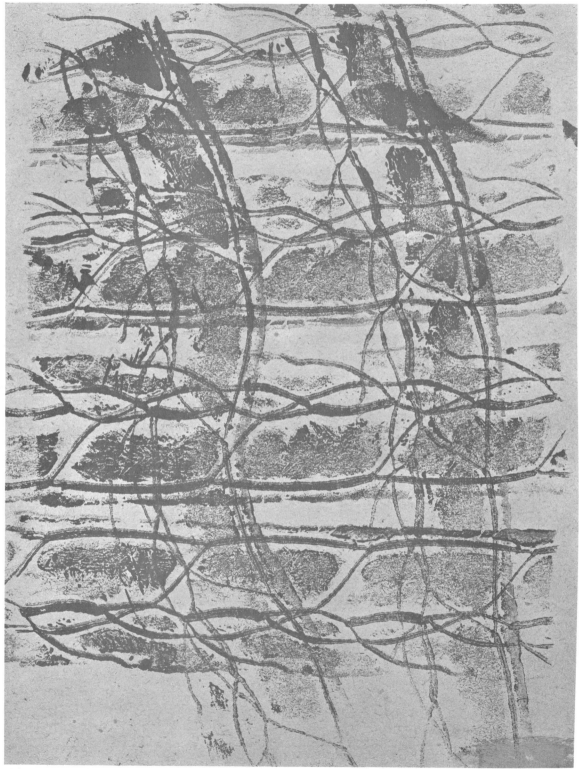

152b

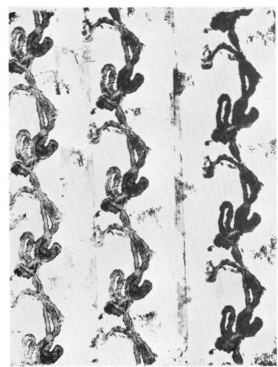

153b

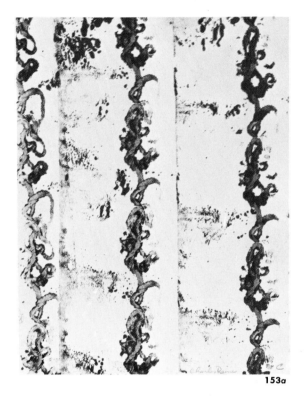

153a

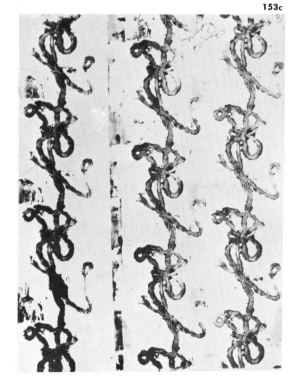

153c

to the roller and exerting less pressure in printing while the line and mass design was achieved by applying more ink and stronger pressure. The unusual results obtained in the design shown in Figure 152b came about by printing straight rows of designs with a well-inked roller and great pressure and then with the same amount of inking and pressure, rolling the design crosswise in a wavy motion.

Figure 153a shows a design formed by tieing a loose bow on the cord, rolling over with an inked roller, applying ink, and then making the impression. The cord was taken off, rolled on again, inked and another impression made, as shown in Figure 153b. Figure 153c is still another result obtained by repeating the process.

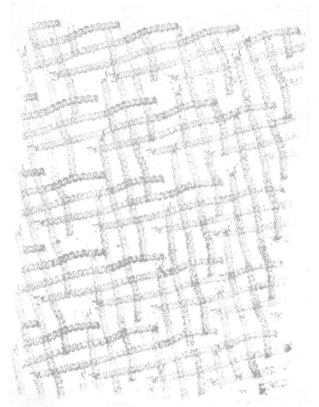

154

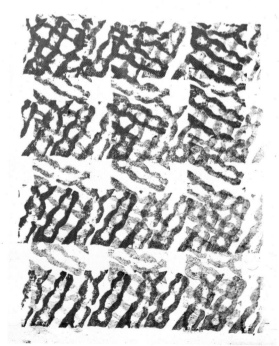

155

Figure 154 is an example of an over-all design printed after pieces of upholstery trimming material were rolled on a paper cylinder that had been coated with rubber cement. Ink was applied and the impression made. In this surface pattern the design was rolled in two different directions. The delicate wavy pattern in the material gives a shimmering effect while the different values give a three-dimensional effect suggesting a rolling movement.

An interesting experiment was made by cutting a rubber tube, approximately ½ inch in diameter, in half with a pair of scissors along a wavy line. The tube was then folded lengthwise and irregular shapes were cut out along the folded edge. Two such designs were cut and glued to the roller. After the ink was applied, the roller design was gently rolled over the paper. A second impression was made in another direction, and the result of this experiment can be seen in Figure 155. This is a more solid design and has a heavier "feel" to it.

156a

156b

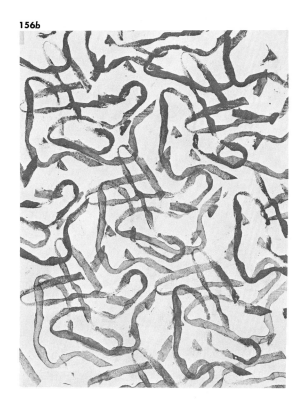

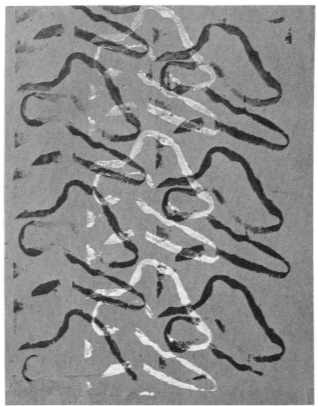

156c

156d

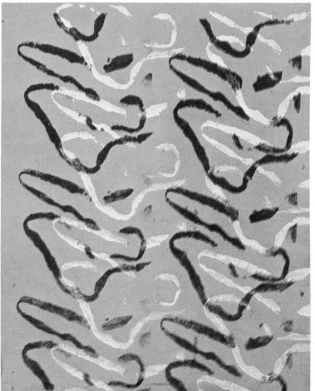

The design in the experiment shown in Figure 156a was made by cutting a thin strip from a rubber tube and gluing it on the rubber roller. Figure 156b is the same design rolled diagonally across the paper one way and then crisscrossed. This gave the design a rather busy effect. Figure 156c is another variation of overlapping two rows of designs in the middle along a vertical line. Two different colors were used. Figure 156d is still another variation. This time each row was overlapped with the same design, using a different color.

A clean, fresh-looking surface pattern was created by cutting and tearing a design out of a piece of foam rubber, gluing it on a paper tube, and applying tempera color with a brush over the design and making the impression at random. The result can be seen in Figure 157. A rather free-looking surface pattern was produced and dark gray and green colors were used.

Many of these designs could be used for objects in the home or industry, such as for textile designs, wallpaper, and floor coverings, to mention but a few. The cylinder is widely used in industry for printing. A field trip to the newspaper in a large city would be a rewarding experience for students. They could learn how effectively this method of printing has been developed and see some of the variations of it such as the offset method and others used in modern printing houses.

As with previous projects, the bulletin boards were used to put up pupils' work for class discussion and evaluation. In some cases the designs were tacked on with a fold to save space and we could see how the designs would appear if they were used as textile designs. This can be seen in Figure 158.

The designs were evaluated in terms of how unusual and different they were in relation to other designs. They were also evaluated in terms of the number of interesting variations produced. Some designs were evaluated in terms of the purpose for which the student intended them. With regard to the individual, the designs were evaluated in terms of how much satisfaction the

157

student derived from expressing his own ideas and feelings.

In summarizing the experiments in this chapter, we may conclude that although many of the ways of printing were used centuries ago, some of the experiments were discoveries insofar as many of the students were concerned. These discoveries were real experiences and a thrill for the boys and girls. Discoveries were made by experimenting with a variety of materials, tools, and processes.

We found that a design may be greatly altered by making only a few changes such as printing in different directions; applying more or less ink or pressure; printing in straight and curved lines; overlapping designs; using different colors; and changing the position of the material on the roller.

We discovered that the designs looked heavier by making them more solid. They could appear lighter and more delicate by varying the thickness of the material used. We learned that we could also use a roller to make random impressions which made the design look less stiff and regimented.

Making impressions with the use of a roller has many possibilities, and teachers should encourage pupils to experiment with a great variety of materials. The experiments in this chapter show the use of printing with a raised surface or as it is sometimes referred to, intaglio. There are also many possibilities of using the roller to print incised or cut-in designs either by using a roller made of soft material that can be easily cut into or by applying some soft plastic material over the roller and carving into it. There are also possibilities of printing with rollers used for painting walls and ceilings. Perhaps a resistant such as a grease pencil could be used over a felt roller which could then be rolled over water-soluble ink and impressions made. That part of the design with the markings made by the grease pencil would resist the watercolor and would appear the color of the paper when the impression was made.

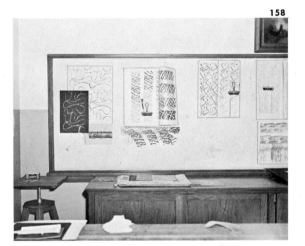

158

159

CHAPTER 12

Designs Created With Assorted Vegetables

Rewarding results were obtained by printing with vegetables. They come in a great variety of types, shapes, textures, sizes, and colors. Because of this variety, they presented an opportunity for pupils at practically all grade levels to discover many and varied ways of printing and understanding design.

The vegetables used for the experiments shown in this chapter included potatoes, cucumbers, carrots, cabbage, corn, green peppers, and pears.

A large, flat table to work on was appreciated by the pupils. Ink rollers, glass plate, printers' ink, colored construction paper, and other kinds of paper of different weight, color, and texture were used. India ink, colored inks, tempera colors and watercolor brush, apron, clean rags, kitchen knives, and block printing gouges provided most of the materials and tools needed.

Figure 159 shows some of the materials which were used. The boys and girls seemed to team up and work in pairs or small groups. This was encouraged, for the pupils seemed to learn a great deal about design by observing one another at work. At times, a healthy competitive spirit prevailed.

Placing additional wastebaskets in accessible places helped to simplify cleaning up. Since a con-

siderable amount of wastepaper accumulated
during the time the pupils experimented, they
were encouraged to dispose of any paper that
was of no use or value to them before the work
area became cluttered.

160

161

Figure 160 shows an experiment made by a junior high school pupil to help him become better acquainted with the use of a cucumber for printing. The top row in Figure 160 shows an impression made by first cutting the cucumber straight across with a knife. This shape represents a cross section or end grain of the cucumber. India ink was brushed on and four impressions were made. It can be observed that as each impression was made it become lighter in value with a slightly different texture.

The second row of impressions shows a change in shape and texture when compared with the first row. This shape was made by cutting across the cucumber with a knife at a slight angle. The shape in the third row from the top was made by increasing the angle of the cut when cutting across the grain of the cucumber. The two shapes at the bottom of Figure 160 were impressions made by cutting the remaining pieces of cucumber lengthwise down the center. Upon close observation the shape of the cucumber seeds can be seen, as

162 163

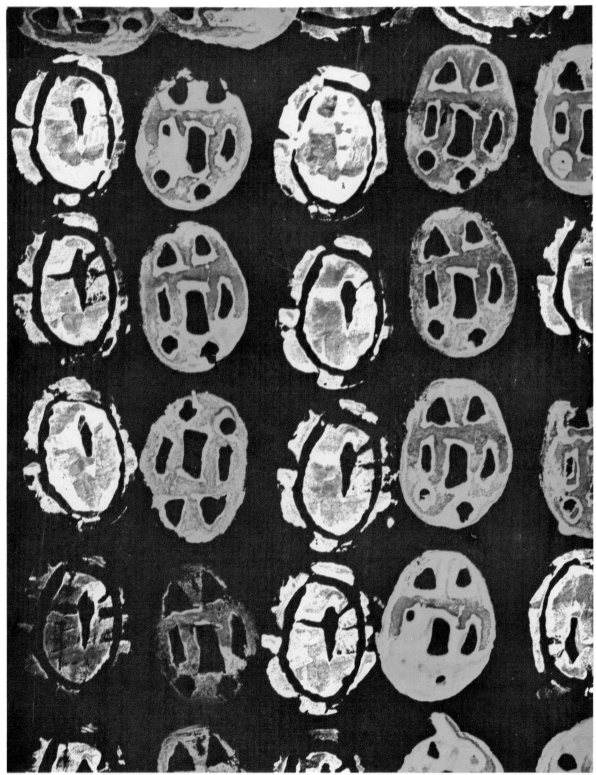

well as the texture of the fleshy part of the cucumber.

Since a large percentage of the cucumber is water, some of the impressions look and feel watery or washed out.

Figure 161 is a simple design of a figure created by making "V" cuts from the outer edge of the cucumber inward toward the center. The watery impression seems to give the design a three-dimensional effect.

Figure 162 is a bold composition made by a junior high school pupil. This design was accomplished by cutting lengthwise through the middle of a carrot. India ink was applied to the carrot and the design printed. The natural shape of the carrot was used and the impressions made indicate the fibrous texture of the vegetable.

Figure 163 is a composition made by the same student. The natural shape of the carrot was altered somewhat by cutting a sharper point and notching the base of the carrot to produce a spearhead design. X's were cut into the carrot at graded intervals. The student cut the X's with a kitchen knife held at a slight angle. Two cuts were made at different angles to make a line.

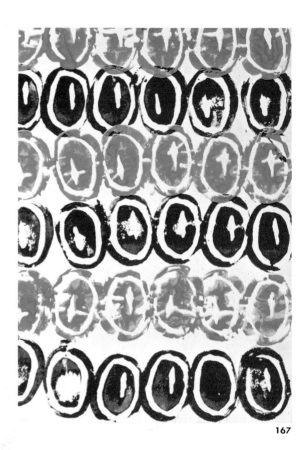

167

In other words, the cutout part of the design is V-shaped. The fibrous texture of the carrot produced varied broken lines in the design which gives a feeling of forward motion as if in flight. This is appropriate since the design resembles a spearhead.

Figure 164 is an over-all design printed by a 4th grade pupil. The design was cut out with a gouge after a potato had been cut in half. The outside shape is the natural shape of the potato. Green tempera color was applied to the potato with a watercolor brush.

Figure 165 shows an over-all design also printed by a 4th grader. Two different designs were used, one on each half of the potato. The designs were printed in yellow and green on black construction paper. Although the impressions are not too clear, the irregularities seem to give the whole pattern a naive and charming effect.

Figures 166 and 167 are prints made by an elementary grade student, showing other variations of designs printed with potatoes. All of these potato prints were made by incising the design and may be referred to as intaglio.

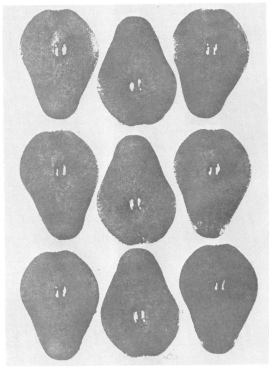

168

169

170

113

Figure 168 is an over-all pattern made by a 7th grade pupil. The design is the natural shape of a pear cut in half. Red-purple ink was applied to the pear with a small brush, and the impressions were made by alternating the position of the pear when printing. The two white or paper-colored dots, which are made by the cavities

formed when the seeds were removed, make the design appear like a mask with a spooky expression.

In Figure 169 the natural shape of the pear was altered by cuts made along the edge and three V-cuts made into the surface of the pear, radiating from a point in the base. Figure 170 shows the use of the same pear design in a different

composition in which four impressions of the design radiate from one point to create another larger design.

Experiments with cabbage prints proved to be an intriguing adventure for junior high school students. Figure 171 shows impressions made by a large outer leaf of a cabbage. A roller was used to apply water-soluble printing ink over the leaf. The impression was made by placing the leaf on a large piece of manila paper and gently pressing it with the fingertips as shown in Figure 159. The veining in each half of the cabbage leaf radiates from a center line. This and other types of radiation are common in many objects found in nature.

A half of a cabbage leaf was used to produce the over-all print shown in Figure 172. This leaf was peeled from the head of cabbage and is smaller than the outer leaf used in Figure 171. As more leaves were peeled, they got smaller although the general appearance of the leaves did not change much. Here was an example of gradation in size as related to the growth and development of an object of nature.

As the pupils peeled off the leaves, they got closer to the core of the cabbage where the leaves were more solidly and firmly packed. One of the pupils cut the remaining cabbage in half and with these two cross sections printed the unusual design in two colors shown in Figure 173. The brown and green water-soluble printing ink, which was used, was applied with a roller.

Corn was a wonderful vegetable to print with. After removing the husk and silk, the cob with its rows of graded, shiny kernels looked as if it had been especially designed for printing.

Figure 174 shows the result obtained by a high school student. To facilitate printing, the student drove two large nails into the ends of the cob and used these as handles. Ink was applied by rolling the corn over the ink which was evenly spread over a piece of 9 by 12 inch glass. Two colors were used; brown color was superimposed over green. After inking, the corn was pressed gently against the paper and rocked back and forth.

In Figure 175 the inked corn was rolled across the width of the paper. As a result, the print appears darker at the beginning and gradually fades out. Because the kernels are larger at one end and the center and get smaller at the other end, the center part of the design appears darker and fades away at either end; however, more so at the end where the kernels were smaller. For contrast the student used part of the husk to print with. The long, fiber-like streaks of the husk printed in red, together with the brown elliptical dot impressions of the kernel produced a very pleasing effect.

The over-all surface pattern shown in Figure 176 is more or less an elaboration of the pattern illustrated in Figure 175. In Figure 176, the same student introduced another design which was printed with a cross section of a green pepper.

The unusual designs that were created by printing with vegetables could be used for wallpaper, wrapping paper, shawls, dress designs, bedspread designs, and linoleum designs to mention a few.

Because printing with vegetables was such an exciting and enjoyable experience for the students, that in itself made it a worthwhile project when we evaluated our efforts. Pupils got excellent results because vegetables make good designs and success was almost certain. Nothing makes more for success than success.

To summarize the work in this chapter we may begin by emphasizing that we learned to appreciate the many different kinds and shapes of vegetables, as well as their textural qualities.

Radiation and gradation were clearly evident in the structural design of many vegetables and in their growth, especially as evidenced in the use of the cabbage for printing. We also learned more about contrast in value, shapes, and color.

The natural shapes of the vegetables made fascinating designs. These were elaborated in some cases by cutting into the vegetable along the outside edge inward and by cutting V-shapes to produce lines in the surface of the printing area

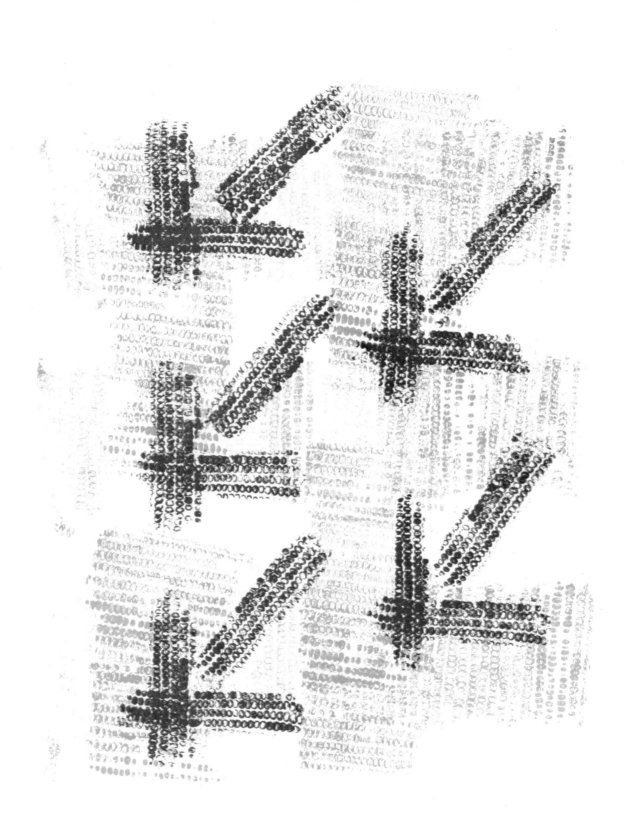

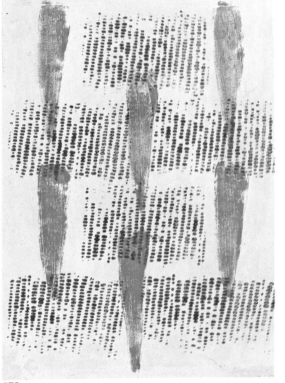

175

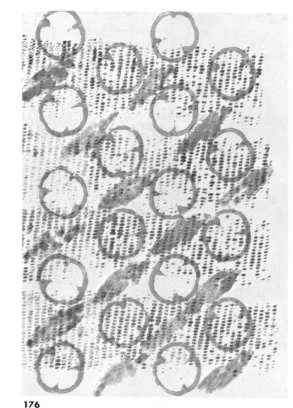

176

of the vegetable. This cutting into, or incising, is sometimes referred to as intaglio.

Many of the students learned to appreciate the rather rough, naive prints made by children in the lower grades. These prints often had a great deal of freedom to them as well as charm.

A word of caution is offered to teachers. Vegetables are perishable and do not stand up as well in the printing process as things of more substantial materials so that the work, of necessity, must move along quickly. Since vegetables are composed of a high percentage of water, some of them have a tendency to be messy to work with. It is advisable that pupils wear aprons or other protective covering. Pupils should be instructed to complete their projects in one period and dispose of the used vegetables, preferably by first wrapping them up in scrap paper.

177

CHAPTER 13

Linear Designs Created With Stencils
and Other Materials

Interesting designs were made by high school pupils using mimeograph stencils. As so often noticed, high school pupils sometimes seem to lack freedom and spontaneity which is characteristic of elementary pupils' work. One of the aims of this project was to stimulate the high school pupils in that direction. Figure 177 shows some of the materials, tools, and equipment which were used.

In an effort to have high school pupils get more spontaneity and freedom in their designs, they were shown examples of Henri Matisse's work, for he has made countless agile line drawings which capture in a few deft strokes the grace and movement of the subject he is drawing.

They were also shown experiments of pre-school and 1st grade children to give them some appreciation and ideas. Pupils in the lower elementary grades and at the pre-school level enjoy expressing themselves with lines, and sometimes it seems that their work has less restraint than that of pupils in the upper grades and high school.

Figure 178 shows several line drawings made by a pre-school girl with a large grease crayon.

Figure 179 shows simple experiments of string design impressions made by a 1st grader. In this experiment, the pupil held a string or cord above a piece of paper and gently lowered it while carefully guiding it to form a design. Another piece of paper was placed over the string design and rubbed with the broad side of a piece of crayon. Sometimes more than one color was used.

Figure 180 is an example of printing with a string dipped in tempera paint. Small pieces of string of various lengths were dipped in paint by a 1st grade student and dropped on a piece of 12 by 18 inch paper. The string was removed after a few seconds.

Figure 181 gives examples of doodle designs made by high school pupils after viewing the above-mentioned experiments and others which were exhibited to the class. It can be noted that the largest of the three designs shows experimentation with three values—white, middle value, and black. It was not long before the entire class was experimenting with doodle designs. The idea of reproducing or printing doodle designs without losing too much of the spontaneity of the line was

178

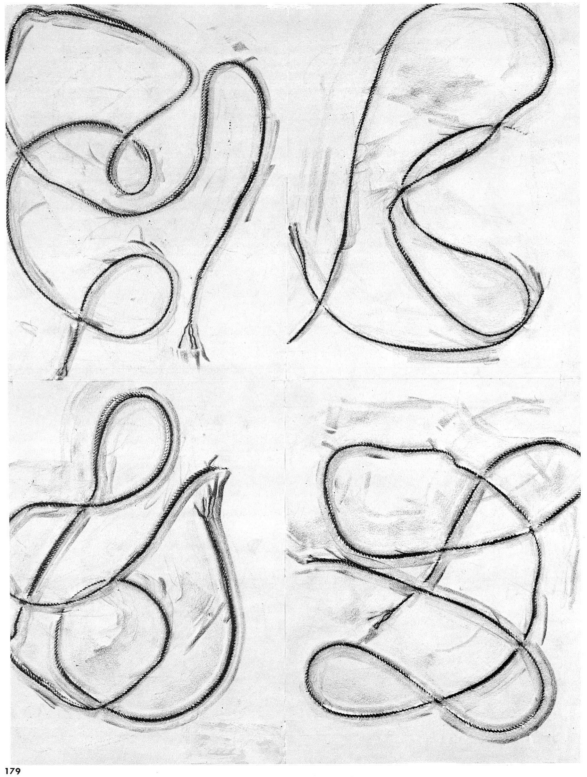

180

a real challenge to the class. One of the pupils who was also taking typing decided to experiment with mimeograph stencils.

The materials used for this experiment were standard mimeograph stencils, a stylus, a roller, a piece of 9 by 12 inch glass, an assortment of paper, mimeograph ink, pencils, pen, India ink, and clean rags.

Mimeograph stencils are approximately 8½ by 16½ inches in size, with a coating of wax-like film over transparent or semitransparent tough paper. Designs were scratched out with any one of the many different standard styli. A sharp pencil also did an effective job. When incising the design, only enough pressure was exerted to remove the wax-like film, leaving the paper under the film intact. This was not a difficult task and with a little practice the students caught on readily.

A lighted glass table-type easel was helpful when incising the design as shown in Figure 177 although it was not absolutely necessary. Some pupils taped the stencils on the classroom windows and got good results. They drew their designs with a soft pencil. Other pupils, who cut their stencils at their desks, outlined their pencil drawings with India ink. This made them transparent enough so that no light was needed.

181

When the doodle designs were drawn, they were placed between the lightweight cardboard backing and the film, which is usually blue. After some experience in doodling, many students worked directly on the stencil without the use of a design to trace. The advantage of working directly on the stencil is that the work seems to be

183a

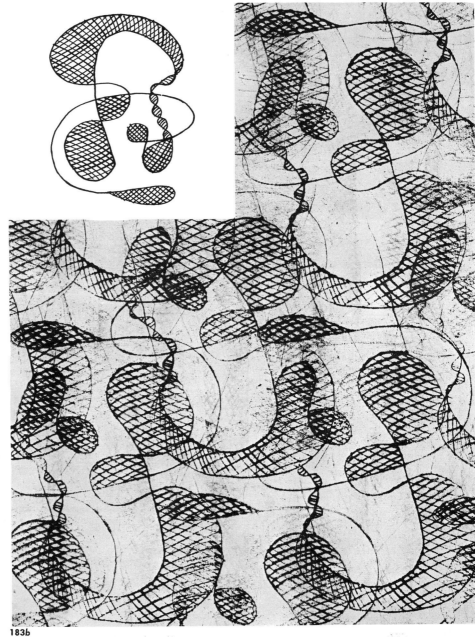

183b

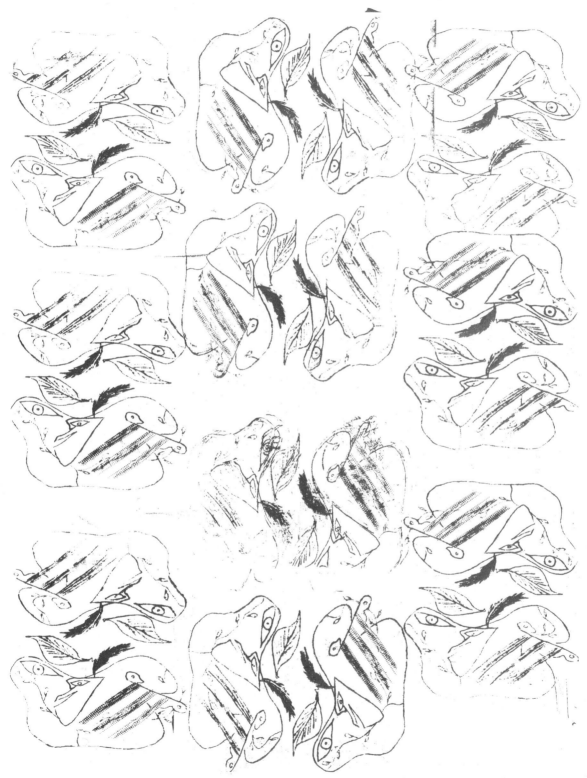

184

185

186

more spontaneous and free. It appears that the more a design is traced, the less life it has.

Students developed a variety of ways and combinations of making doodles. One pupil made a free form similar to the string design, outlined it with India ink, and then included independent subordinate forms inside of the outline and achieved a halftone by stippling. The inside halftone forms were of different sizes and similar, harmonious shapes, which gives the design a rhythmic feeling. Figure 182a is an example of this type of doodle. Figure 182b is an over-all pattern using the same design.

The printing of the over-all pattern was done by placing the cut stencil, blue sheet only, over a large sheet of white drawing paper and going over it with an inked roller. Mimeograph printing ink was used. Upon observation, it can be noted that the design was overlapped. As a result of the overlapping, another value was introduced into the pattern. The intermediate value in the stencil design was made with a standard transparent plastic shading plate. No guide lines were used when printing.

Figure 183a is another variation of the doodle. In this design the student achieved a rhythmic effect in the intermediate value by filling in the loops with crosshatch lines, which were done freehand on the stencil. This design was overlapped to form the pattern shown in Figure 183b.

Figure 184 is an experiment in using red color instead of black ink. The arrangement of the overall pattern is quite different from either Figures 182b or 183b.

At the 6th-grade level doodle warm-up exercises were conducted. Later, the pupils were asked to draw animals in motion. Figure 185 is an animated drawing of deer jumping over logs. In this design, which may be adapted to mimeograph printing, some of the fluidity and freedom that is evident in doodles appears to have been carried over to the design. The fish designs in Figure 186 are the result of similar experiments conducted at the high school level. The lines in these designs seem to be flowing uninterruptedly, adding animation to the designs.

When looking at over-all doodle design patterns created by printing with mimeograph stencils, one is reminded of Far East or Near East fabric designs. Mimeograph prints may be put to use for wallpaper designs, tablecloths, shawls, upholstery materials, wall decorations, and wrapping paper.

When evaluating the pupils' work, we thought in terms of how much appeal the design had, originality, and finally, how well it was printed. This involved the technical aspects of reproduction. In evaluating the work, class participation is very important, for it helps to bring about better understanding of design through discussion and usually helps to instill class enthusiasm.

In summarizing the work presented in this chapter we may conclude that line designs that are free and spontaneous seem to have "life" in them. This may be achieved by working directly on the stencil. The more the design is traced, the less spontaneity it seems to have.

To achieve a degree of freedom and originality it is a good idea to work with tools and materials that can aid us; for example, a piece of charcoal, a soft pencil, a large wax crayon or a piece of string. Doodling is an excellent way to get started.

We learned that there can be a great variety in doodle designs, and the stencil designs can be done in different values as well as different colors. We can sense rhythm in the design not only in the shapes and forms used but also through the repetition of values and colors. Overlapping a design may sometimes add interest because new forms seem to emerge as well as another value. However, it helps to keep the design simple and limit it to not more than four values or colors.

Similar shapes, although they may vary in size, seem to add harmony to the design.

Although printing with mimeograph stencils is a very fascinating and exciting experience, it is rather messy. Teachers should caution students to wear a smock or apron to prevent soiling of clothes. When printing, it is advisable to first cover the desks or work tables with plently of old newspapers or other protective material. Clean rags are almost a "must" to keep the hands clean so as not to soil the printed page.

187

Designs Created From Reliefs Made of Assorted Materials, Paraffin, Plaster, Linoleum and Wood

In this chapter we will describe and show many designs done by pupils at different grade levels with a variety of materials. These materials are mentioned in the title of this chapter. In addition, we will discuss and show designs printed in a variety of ways with some of the materials used. Figure 187 shows some of the materials used in one of the projects which will be mentioned later.

The materials used in the first project which had to do with designs printed with reliefs made of assorted materials, included such things as buttons, pieces of burlap, cloth of various tetxures, toothpicks, seeds, coarse sandpaper, rubber bands, stones, string, sequins, pieces of curtain fabric, lace, shells, 9 by 12 inch pieces of newsboard or any other cardboard, tempera colors, glue, and shellac.

This project includes the work of pupils from grades 1—6. They gathered assorted scrap materials with interesting textural qualities, shapes, and sizes and worked toward harmonious, exciting, abstract compositions.

Each child was given a piece of 9 by 12 inch newsboard on which he began to arrange his composition with the scrap materials he brought. After some experimentation the final design was decided upon and glued to the cardboard. In some cases the pupil overlapped the materials to

188a

get unusual effects. Others superimposed seeds, buttons, and other objects on fabric. There were as many different ways of handling and arranging the material as there were children in the class.

After the glue dried, the relief design was given a coat or two of shellac. When using shellac, we made sure that it was fresh. Shellac that has been stored several months does not dry hard and remains tacky whereas fresh shellac will dry in an hour or two.

When the shellac dried, the relief design was ready to print with. This was an exciting time for the children. Tempera colors were brushed on the relief design, and a trial print was made on news-print paper. A number of pupils brought old pillowcases and used this material to print on. Some pupils used textile inks on the cloth to give the design more permanence.

A surprising amount of variety was evident in the use of materials and the arrangement of the designs. The print, Figure 188a was made on cloth from the relief design and shown in Figure 188b. The design was composed of scraps of corduroy material, onion bag, string, buttons, and other materials.

188b

Figures 189a and 189b show a relief design and print in which the following materials were used: scraps of corduroy, overlapped; buttons and watermelon seeds; and cotton cloth. This design is heavier in appearance, with the emphasis on mass rather than on line. To achieve this, more paint was used and greater pressure was applied when printing.

Some pupils brought cotton curtains and aprons from home and printed interesting surface patterns using this method.

Figure 190 is a design printed by a junior high school pupil on an old pillowcase. The same method was used as by the elementary grade pupils with the exception that the pupil used only cardboard cutouts and string for this composition. By using only two materials the design appears to be less busy and have more definition and strength.

189a

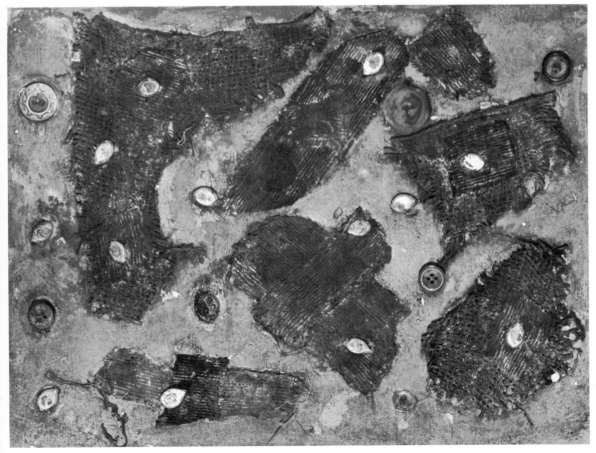

Inspired by successes in printing with a variety of materials, the high school students decided to try using blocks of paraffin. The object of these experiments was to see how effectively designs could be made by working with a very impressionable material.

The materials and tools used were canning paraffin, which comes in blocks 2½ by 6 by ⅝ inch in size, wire screen, a baren, spoon, pencil, gouges, pins, roller, printing paper, inks, and tempera colors. Some of these materials and tools can be seen in Figure 187.

Steps 1, 2, 3, and 4 in Figure 191 show the procedure of preparing the paraffin, drawing the design, transferring the design to the paraffin, and finally, cutting the design. Larger designs may be made by melting the paraffin over a slow fire and pouring it into the desired size pan. Enough wax should be used to make the plate about ¾ inch thick.

Steps 5 and 6 in Figure 192 show how to get the paraffin block ready for printing and making the print.

Since a simple baren, which has been used by the Japanese and Chinese for centuries, proves effective in this project, instructions on how to make one are shown in Figure 193.

Almost any kind of paper may be used to print on. However, Japanese rice paper proved to be best. Any kind of printers' ink may be used but water-soluble ink is easier to clean up. Tempera color may also be used.

Figures 194 and 195 show some of the unusual results obtained. The experiment in the upper right-hand corner of Figure 195 shows an interesting effect produced by pressing a wire screen into the wax and then removing it. Pupils used similar prints for post cards and book plates.

Teachers should instruct pupils to use care in storing the paraffin blocks. A cool place, away from heat or sunlight, should be used. An excessive amount of heat will soften the paraffin and diffuse the lines. Paraffin blocks should be stored by placing them on edge and not one on top of another.

Another method which is similar to printing with paraffin is the use of plaster of Paris. The differ-

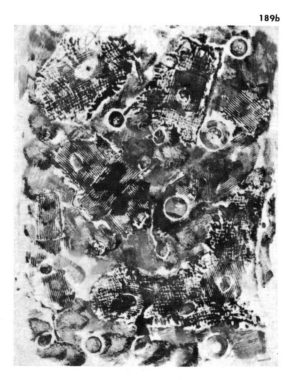

189b

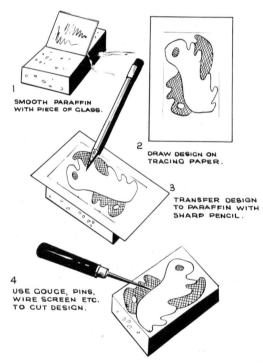

1 SMOOTH PARAFFIN WITH PIECE OF GLASS.

2 DRAW DESIGN ON TRACING PAPER.

3 TRANSFER DESIGN TO PARAFFIN WITH SHARP PENCIL.

4 USE GOUGE, PINS, WIRE SCREEN ETC. TO CUT DESIGN.

191

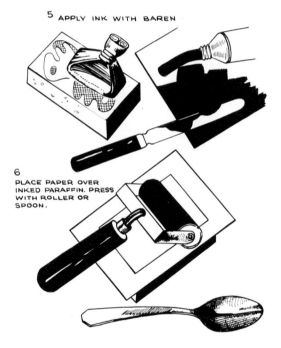

5 APPLY INK WITH BAREN

6 PLACE PAPER OVER INKED PARAFFIN. PRESS WITH ROLLER OR SPOON.

192

A SIMPLE BAREN

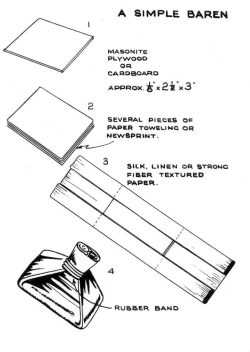

1

MASONITE
PLYWOOD
OR
CARDBOARD

APPROX. $\frac{1}{8}"$ x $2\frac{1}{2}"$ x $3"$

2

SEVERAL PIECES OF
PAPER TOWELING OR
NEWSPRINT.

3

SILK, LINEN OR STRONG
FIBER TEXTURED
PAPER.

4

RUBBER BAND

193

ence is that plaster of Paris blocks are more permanent and can take more abuse. Sharper and stronger tools, preferably made of metal, are needed.

One of the aims of the pupils at the high school level was to experiment with this material in order to understand better how this material behaves. The pupils wished to learn some of the advantages and disadvantages and to discover how they could best express themselves with it.

Figure 196 shows the materials which are needed and a step-by-step setup on how to get started. The materials shown in Figure 196 include the following: a glass or metal plate, plasticene, two parts of plaster of Paris and one part of water (shown in water mixing pans), paper for printing, knives, gouges, ink, and a roller.

The first step in getting started was to select a piece of glass or a flat metal piece large enough to meet the size requirements of the design to be cut. A piece of plasticene was rolled to form a round rod approximately ¾ inch in diameter.

194

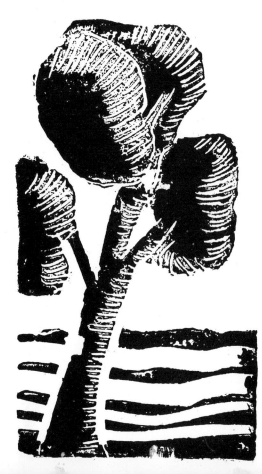

This was then placed on the glass plate and formed to the shape desired. The plasticene was pressed down and spread out a little at the base so it would adhere better to the glass and make a waterproof seam.

Two parts of plaster of Paris to one part of water made a good mixture. Because plaster of Paris hardens quickly, small amounts were mixed at a time and poured into the form until the desired thickness was built up. After the plaster of Paris was poured, the glass was shaken and tapped gently against the table with an up and down motion. This helped to do away with any air bubbles which might have formed while the material was being poured. Although it takes several months before the plaster of Paris is completely dry and hardened, after about half an hour it had set and the plasticene form was removed. The plaster of Paris slab was then gently removed from the glass. Some pupils spread a little vaseline on the surface of the glass before pouring the plaster of Paris and this facilitated removing the slab when the plaster had set.

After the slab was removed, it was allowed to dry overnight. The next day pupils began to experiment by cutting into the slab with metal V-shaped and U-shaped gouges. One pupil discovered that it was easier to cut into the slab after soaking it in water for a few seconds. After a little practice cutting and getting the feel of the material, the pupils began to cut out designs.

It was necessary to ink the slab with a roller several times to allow the material to absorb a sufficient amount of ink before an impression could be made. After properly inking the slab with water-soluble ink, the slab was held face up in the left hand and a piece of paper was placed over it with the right hand and gently rubbed with a piece of cloth. After rubbing over the entire design the paper was removed.

Figure 196 shows a pupil inking the slab with a roller. Behind her are some finished prints. Figure 197 shows a finished print made by a student with the center design cut out or incised. The horizontal lines around the design were made by cutting out the background.

Pupils used their prints as wall decorations.

Teachers should caution the pupils that plaster of Paris slabs are brittle and may shatter if dropped. Although pupils enjoy this project very much, the fine dust which results from cutting into the slabs makes for a messy situation. Desks should be cleaned frequently with a damp rag. Soaking the slab in water before carving helps to keep the dust down.

In this part of the chapter, which deals with printing designs with linoleum, we are going to show that cutting linoleum designs is not just a question of using either white or black lines, but rather that there are many and different ways of cutting. The experiments shown encouraged students to practice and become thoroughly acquainted with the peculiarities of different tools; to handle them effectively; and to produce a variety of techniques, distinctly their own, which they could use to express themselves. We also wish to show that cuts made with tools sometimes harmonized with certain subjects and by varying the size and direction of the cuts, different kinds of action and texture were produced. We will also discuss and show finished linoleum prints which express the feeling or mood of the subject involved.

The materials used in these projects consisted of linoleum cutting tools of different sizes and shapes such as knives, V-shaped and narrow and wide U-shaped gouges, chisels, a carpenter's steel square, a triangle, a small carborundum stone for sharpening the cutting tools, a cutting board, paper, inks, roller, battleship linoleum, tracing paper, tacks, and other common art materials.

We found that one of the best ways to get started was to become acquainted with some of the materials, tools, and processes involved. Some pupils purchased kits which included about six different sizes and shapes of gouges and other cutting tools which were inserted into a holder, similar to the way a pen point is inserted. Linoleum was purchased from department stores at a nominal cost. It is interesting to point out that professional printers found that a well-cut linoleum block can be printed as many as 100,000 times before it shows any signs of wear. Commercially prepared linoleum blocks can be purchased in any art supply store. These are usually mounted on ¾

195

inch plywood. Some of these blocks are light gray or white, which is helpful when tracing the design on the block. Scrap linoleum, purchased from department stores, may be mounted although it was found not to be absolutely necessary. The pupils discovered that if they warmed the linoleum over a heater for a while it was easier to cut.

Figure 198 shows some experiments made by pupils to get acquainted with some techniques of handling the cutting tools.

Figure 199 also shows some of the tools which were used in cutting and a cutting board. The cutting board was approximately 5 inches wide, 13 inches long, and ¾ inch thick, made of pine. It had two additional pieces of wood, 5 inches long, 1½ inches wide, and ¾ inch thick, nailed at either end of the board, one on each side. The end pieces were each fastened with three nails.

196

197

198

DIFFERENT TOOLS &
HANDLING PRODUCE
VARIED TECHNIQUES

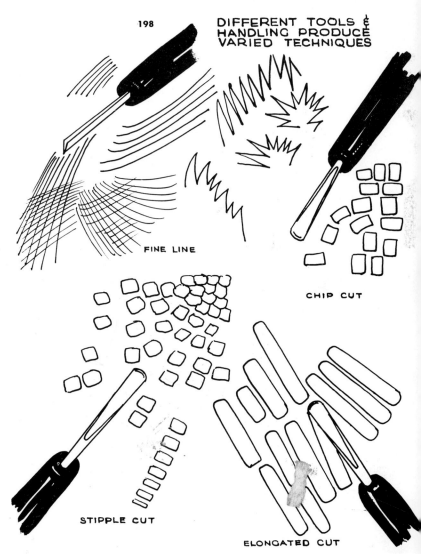

FINE LINE

CHIP CUT

STIPPLE CUT

ELONGATED CUT

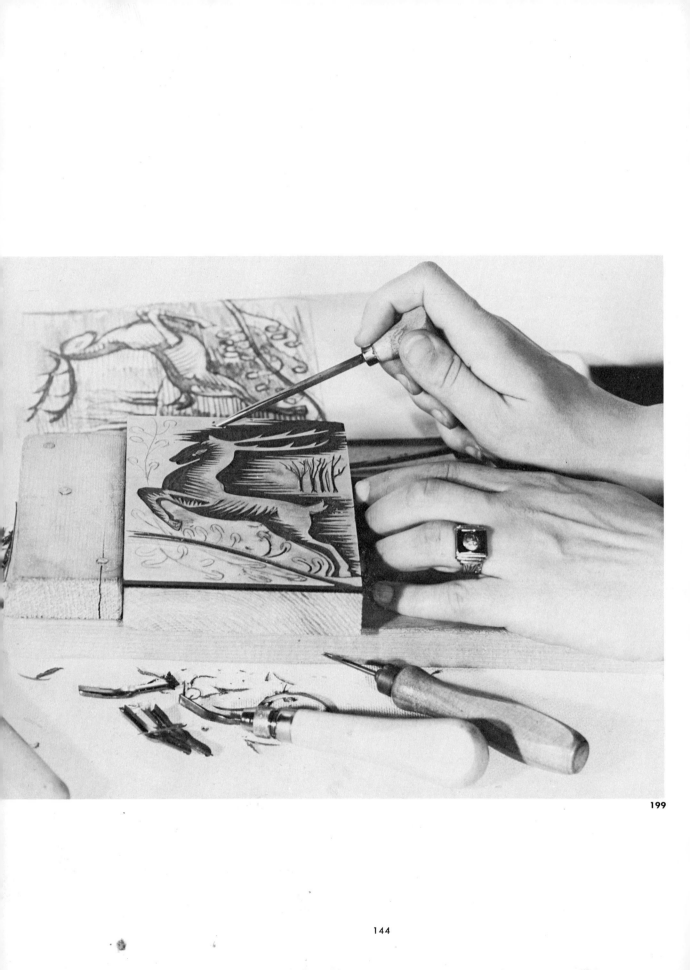

This piece of equipment was easily and inexpensively made and was well worth the time, for it proved to be a valuable safety aid. One end piece was placed against the table and the other, as shown in Figure 199, was used to press the block against when cutting.

Since the tools are very sharp, teachers should caution the pupils about the danger involved if the tools are not used properly. Students were impressed to keep two things in mind; first, to use the cutting board to keep the block securely in place, and secondly, to cut away from them-

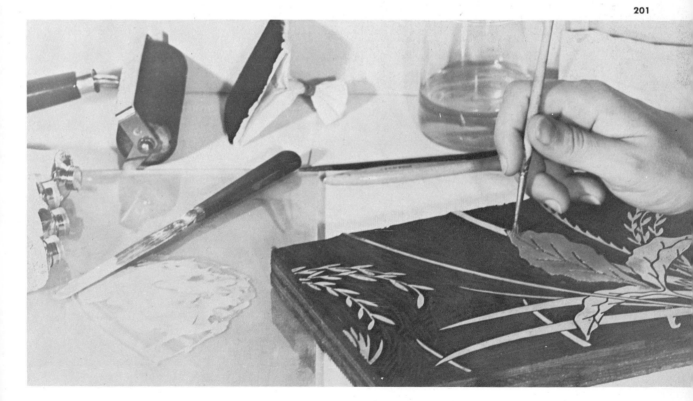

Donald K   Delevan

203

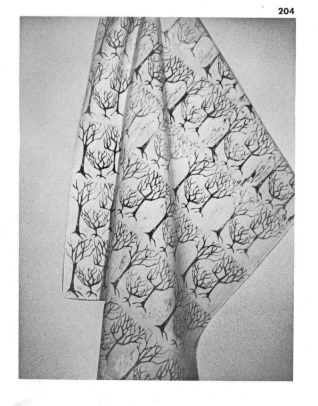

204

selves when using the linoleum cutting tools. A small first-aid kit was kept handy, for it seemed that no matter how much advise and emphasis was placed on proper handling of sharp tools, someone in the class always nicked his finger.

When cutting into a large piece of linoleum, as shown in Figure 200, it is not necessary to use a cutting board as the pressure of the left hand on the linoleum while cutting is sufficient to keep it in place.

After a little practice and experimentation, the pupils soon became acquainted with the materials, tools, and some of the processes and were ready to cut out designs. The designs were planned and sketched in pencil on paper, then transferred in reverse to the linoleum. Some pupils sketched directly with a grease pencil as shown in Figure 200. After some experience in cutting out designs, pupils were able to turn out excellent designs by cutting directly without the use of sketches.

Usually, when cutting out solid designs, a very sharp knife or a V-shaped gouge was used to cut along the outline to a depth of about 1/32 inch to 1/16 inch, depending upon the size and intricacy of the design. Then, all portions which were not to be printed were cut away with a chisel or a U-shaped gouge. Care was taken that the edges of the design were clean and sharp with no undercuts. Undercuts may result in a soft impression which soon loses definiteness, or they may cause chipping.

There are two methods of cutting out line designs, the black line and the white line. The black line is one in which all the spaces between the lines of the design are cut or gouged out. Two or more cuts are needed to produce a single black line. This is also known as the relief method. To produce a white line a single cut may be made. This is sometimes referred to as the intaglio method.

Designs were made either in one of the three ways described or in a combination of two or three methods. Tempera colors, oil-base, or water-soluble printing inks were applied to the blocks with a roller, a baren as illustrated in Figure 193, or a brush, as shown in Figure 201.

Printing was done in one of four ways. First, by placing a piece of paper over the inked block and rubbing it with a burnisher or the bowl of

205a

205b

205c

205d

206

a spoon with enough pressure to make the paper pick up the ink. This is sometimes referred to as the Japanese method. Secondly, small blocks were pressed against the paper with the hand or foot. Thirdly, large blocks were placed in a screw-type press. Finally, when many copies were needed, the blocks were sent to a commercial printer.

When pressing by hand or when using the screw-type press, several sheets of paper were used to form a padding. Sometimes, in spite of the amount of padding used, the blocks printed light in certain areas. This indicated unevenness in the block itself. To overcome this defect, a print was made on a very thin piece of paper. The parts which were too light were cut out and pasted on the corresponding spot on the back of the block and another print pulled. If necessary, other cuttings were made and pasted until an even print was made.

Pupils experimented on a variety of different

207

208a

208b

208c

208d

208e

209

kinds of colored and textured papers and textiles to get unusual and interesting effects. Figure 202 shows an over-all pattern done by a student in junior high school. A brayer with tempera paint was rolled over colored paper. When the paint was dry, a linoleum block was used to print a design over it. The textured effect produced by using the brayer and tempera paint makes it appear as if the design was printed on silk or some other fine material.

Figure 203 illustrates a charming design showing three saints, created by an elementary grade pupil. This print was made on linen and shows the effective use of white and black line to produce textural effects.

A high school pupil printed the striking black line design shown in Figure 204. This design was printed with textile ink on white cotton.

Some students experimented by applying glue to the raised surfaces of the linoleum and then sprinkled on flocking material with a salt shaker. The advantage of applying the flocking was that a more uniform print could be made because the block absorbed more ink or paint.

210

Students also liked to experiment with different subject matter. The character study prints made by high school students, shown in Figure 205, help to point out the different techniques that were used. In Figure 205a, the pupil simply cut out the light pattern and highlights and achieved a dramatic effect. The background was left untouched. In Figure 205b, the pupil used a combination of solid patterns and black lines. In this design the background was cut out. For the portrait of the pilot shown in Figure 205c, the pupil used the background, as well as the subject to add interest. An attempt was made to show roundness by the direction of the lines and a middle value or half-tone as seen in the handling of the lines in the face. A bold effect was created by using solid shapes and lines in the portrait, shown in Figure 205d. Attention was drawn to the background which is, however, subordinated to the dominant part of the composition.

A stained-glass effect was created by a college student in the print shown in Figure 206. Another student made the religious scene shown in Figure 207. The technique used seems to fit the subject

211a

211b

admirably well. The lines seem to express sorrow and suffering.

The linoleum prints shown in Figure 208a, b, c, d, and e were made by former high school pupils and illustrate a variety of techniques used in handling landscapes. Each individual expressed a different feeling about the subject. The print in Figure 208a seems to indicate late Fall and suggests stillness and rest. In Figure 208b, the print seems to speak of desolation, while the one shown in Figure 208c suggests fullness and abundance. The print shown in Figure 208d indicates that it is Spring or early Summer and seems to suggest crispness, freshness, and a feeling of movement. The print in Figure 208e indicates Winter and has a cold, barren feeling to it.

Linoleum prints may be made in a variety of sizes, anywhere from 1 inch square to one that is 18 by 27 inches in size, as the one shown in Figure 209. This is an abstract print entitled "*The Evangelist.*" This abstraction conveys the feeling of the artist about the subject which he chose to design. It is full of drama and excitement. This design was made in three colors by a college student.

An interesting effect of movement was achieved by another college student. As shown in Figure 210, the print was repeated several times. Appropriately enough it is entitled "*Processional.*"

Figure 211a, b, c, and d are examples of the individual steps showing how a three-color block print was made, Figure 211d being the composite print. The original size of this print was 9 by 12 inches. In color printing a block is cut for each color to be printed. In this case Figure 211a represents a yellow print and Figure 211b a purple print. The key block, usually black as shown in Figure 211c, carried the design and was cut first. Offsetting the print of the key block onto the other blocks is the quickest and most accurate method of transferring the design. To offset, a print was made of the key block and a fresh block was placed on the print while it was still wet. It was then run through the press. The result was a lighter but identical print on the second block. Great care was taken to see that the two blocks registered correctly; otherwise, while the prints would be identical, one block would not print exactly on top of the first but to one side or

211c

211d

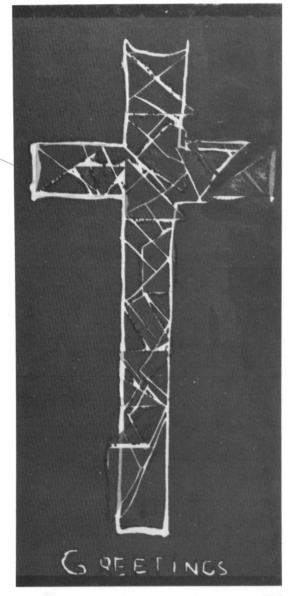

212a

212b

perhaps higher, resulting in a blurred outline in the finished print.

Another way of making a multicolored print was by applying different colors to one block with a small stencil brush.

The hand-printed Christmas cards shown in Figure 212 were made by college freshmen who were not classified as art students. Similar techniques could be employed by junior and senior high school pupils. The clever use of different colors was achieved by pasting together various shaped colored paper and printing over it. The colored paper was cut in long strips, in free forms or definite shapes, and then pasted along an edge, in the center of the design or in little patches throughout the design. Pieces of colored paper were also printed over with different colored ink and then cut into free forms and superimposed on the original design. Sometimes windows were cut out of the design and colored paper pasted in place. This technique offered many opportunities for students to use their imaginations and express their thoughts and ideas.

In this part of the chapter, we will discuss and illustrate some of the methods used to print with wood. Although the pupils preferred to work with linoleum or hard rubber because it was easier to cut in any direction with tools ordinarily found in the art room, they nevertheless were eager to learn something about woodcuts and engravings and gain some appreciation of this material.

Some of the materials discussed in this project were soft woods, knives and gouges, hardwoods, engravers' tools, and the many other tools and materials mentioned in linoleum printing.

Two main divisions in printing with wood were discussed with students in the junior and senior high school. These were prints made from blocks cut with knives and gouges in softwoods and prints made from hardwood blocks cut with engraving tools. The students were reminded that the softwood blocks were usually made of beech, cherry, apple, or pear wood, cut with the grain in blanks about 1 inch thick. The hardwood blocks were usually made of boxwood and were cut across the grain. Very fine lines were cut with engravers' tools. This method of working was used extensively in book and magazine illustrations of the 19th century.

Some confusion exists regarding the terms woodcut and wood engraving. In a woodcut the block is cut with the grain of the wood which frequently shows in the print. Figure 213 shows an example of a woodcut made by a college student entitled "Self Portrait." In this woodcut the student used the natural formation of the grain as part of the design of the character study. He used knives and gouges. The work appears somewhat coarse, the lines heavier, and the black and white areas in broader masses than in a wood engraving. Because the end grain of hardwood can be cut with engravers' tools, fine, crisp, clean-cut lines are characteristic of a wood engraving, as shown in Figure 214. This was made by a contemporary professional artist whose work appears sculpturesque. The title of the print is "By the Grace of God."

As previously mentioned, many prints were used for magazine illustrations. Today, the artist usually cuts and prints his own blocks for exhibition purposes, greeting cards, and book plates. Some are still used for book illustrations.

If teachers wish to experiment with woodcuts and engravings, it is suggested that this be done at the junior and senior high school level since great care is required in the handling of the sharp tools used. Engraving tools are not as yet commonly found in most junior and senior high schools, and it is sometimes necessary for the students to purchase their own tools.

In evaluating the work used in this chapter, considerable emphasis was placed on the pupil's inventiveness and resourcefulness in using new and different ways to express his ideas and feelings.

Some of the work was selected because it helped to clarify some fact or idea when describing pupils' experiences with designing that could benefit the pupil and the class as a whole. Some prints were selected because they were beautiful as pieces of art.

212c

212d

To summarize the pupils' work activities described in this chapter, it should be pointed out that the reliefs made with assorted materials were successfully done from grades 1–12. We learned that reliefs of this kind may be overdone by selecting too many different materials. By using some critical judgement in selecting only a few pieces of material, the designs will tend to have more unity, rhythm, and harmony. On the whole, the design will be less busy. Knowing how much or how little to put into a design to make it appealing is a difficult task and is usually learned through experience.

Paraffin prints may also be made at practically all grade levels. This is a fascinating material to use because it is very impressionable, quick results are obtained, and it is a clean material to work with. The material itself seems to offer a challenge to the pupil's imagination.

The use of plaster to make prints is an absorbing project, for there is a considerable amount of curiosity aroused in the pupils when they prepare the slab. Here they see a powdery material un-dergo a chemical and physical change in a comparatively short time. Although this material was somewhat messy to work with, many exciting designs were created on a variety of shapes which formed part of the design. Other things which could be developed would be to make designs with plasticene, pour the plaster of Paris over it, and when set remove the plasticene from the slab and use the slab to print the design. Can you think of another way that could be used to print with this material?

When discussing linoleum prints considerable emphasis was placed on the care and use of the sharp tools and the danger involved. For this reason it seemed wise to use this method of printing only with junior and senior high school pupils. Because this material can be cut in either direction with ease and is sufficiently strong to take considerable abuse in handling, it proved to be an excellent material through which the children could express themselves. Unique designs were made in white and black line and solid shapes, as well as in combinations of three techniques. We learned

213

214

that students could use linoleum blocks to express charm, desolation, fullness, freshness, tragedy, sorrow, humor, power, and many other feelings and moods with different degrees of intensity as found in everyday life. We learned to cut colored paper in a variety of shapes, paste it in different positions, and print over it to create original designs for greeting cards. We learned to use and appreciate the ways of making prints with several colors.

In our discussions on printing with wood, we learned that woodcuts are made by cutting with the grain of softwood and wood engravings are cut on the end grain of hardwood. Although wood engravings have been replaced by newer methods of reproduction in the field of commercial printing, many artists still use wood as a means of expressing themselves. Unlike woodcuts, wood engravings are distinguished by their freshness of line and crisp, clean-cut character of the print.

CHAPTER 15

Designs Created With Stencils (Serigraphy)

The art of stenciling and similar methods are practically limitless in their scope and may be developed to a very high degree of usefulness. They require a small expenditure of time and money and present a wide field for the individual expression of taste, skill, and experimentation. In this chapter some techniques of stenciling in several mediums upon various surfaces are brought to the attention of the reader. Since the same principles involved in printing with stencils are employed in silk screen printing, or serigraphy, both of these methods are included in this chapter.

Figure 215 shows some of the equipment used in an experiment in serigraphy which will be described later this chapter. In the first project,

which was a spatter print made by a 3rd grader, the following materials were used: flowers, leaves, weeds, wallpaper, an old toothbrush, a piece of wire screen approximately 3 by 3 inches, an old catalog, and tempera colors. Spatter prints may be looked upon as a variation of stenciling. Figure 216 shows the completed spatter print.

The first step in making a spatter print was to place a flower, leaf, or weed into an old catalog and press it by weighing it down with books. While the objects were being pressed, the children experimented with the toothbrush, wire screen, and tempera colors. At first, some pupils had a little difficulty in judging the proper amount of paint to have on the toothbrush and how to use it effectively over the wire screen, but with a little practice, they mastered it.

After the objects were pressed and appeared flat, they were placed on pieces of wallpaper. Wallpaper of different textures, plain or with inconspicuous patterns, was used. The bristles of the toothbrush were then dipped part way into tempera paint and the surplus paint was allowed to drip off. Next, the wire screen was held in the left hand, above the object, and with the toothbrush in the right hand, the pupils gently rubbed the brush against the screen and let the spattered paint fall around the object. The distance of the screen from the object varied, but about 6 inches was good to start with. The farther the screen was from the object, the less concentration of spattered paint. Some pupils applied the tempera paint to the toothbrush with a watercolor brush, as they felt that in this way they could control the amount of paint better.

Empty paper cylindrical gallon cartons from ice cream were decorated with this stenciling method. These made fine wastepaper baskets, and the pupils gave them to their mothers for Mother's Day.

It can be observed that in the above described spattering method the impression of the object was the color of the original background or paper,

216

and the outline of the object was made as a result of spattering paint around it.

In the following experiments made by 3rd grade pupils, the process was the reverse. The following materials were used: pieces of stencil paper approximately 2 ½ by 4 inches, a pair of scissors, a watercolor brush, tempera colors, and colored construction paper.

The pupils were given pieces of stencil paper, and they cut out only one petal of a flower from a piece of stencil paper. From another piece they cut out the center of the flower if they were going to use it. From another piece they cut out a leaf and finally from still another piece they cut out a stem.

A piece of 12 by 18 inch colored construction paper was folded the long way across and then in thirds and opened out flat. The sheet was di-

vided into six squares. Starting with the first square the pupils proceeded to take the stencil with the center of the flower cutout and placed it in the approximate center of the square. With a brush which had been dipped in paint they brushed on the paint from the edge of the cutout, inward. When the paint dried, they took the petal stencil and in a similar manner applied the paint, then gently removed the stencil. When the first petal dried the stencil was placed in another position, paint applied and again the stencil was removed. This was repeated until the desired amount of petals were stenciled. The stem and leaf stencils were used in the same way.

Some pupils worked on one flower at a time, others were successful in working on all six designs. They would first stencil all six centers, then one petal next to the center. By the time they were stenciling the petal on the sixth flower, the first flower was dry and ready for the next petal. Two or three different colors were used in some designs. The finished surface patterns, as shown in Figure 217, made cheerful wall decorations.

Figures 218a, b, c, and d show a variety of ways of using a simple stencil as done by junior high school students. In the surface pattern shown in Figure 218a the pupil used two stencils. The first stencil was used in a manner similar to that described in the spattering method, in that the design was made by the color around it. In this experiment a charcoal sponge was dipped in color, applied to the pattern, and worked outward. The strokes of the charcoal sponge also formed part of the design. After repeating this design in different positions and letting it dry, a second stencil was used. This was a cutout stencil. The paint was again applied with a charcoal sponge but this time it was stroked from the outside of the stencil inward. This design was superimposed over the first design and printed in different positions. Red and brown tempera colors were used.

The surface pattern in Figure 218b was done with one pattern and two different colors, orange and red. The paint was brushed inward with a stiff brush and a flame-like effect was produced.

Figure 218c shows a completed surface pattern created with two different stencils and three colors, reddish-brown, red, and black. The de-

signs are solid and clean-cut and produce an unusual three-dimensional effect with varied movement.

Figure 218d is an interesting experiment showing the stencil printed with a solid edge, and a textured center produced with a brush. The dominant design is interlaced with a subordinate curved line design. Blue, red, and yellow tempera colors were used.

Instead of using scissors to cut out stencils, some of the pupils in the high school preferred a regular stencil knife, as shown in Figure 219a. Clean-cut stencils may be made by using a knife.

The tool must be kept sharp at all times so it is a good idea to keep a small oil stone or a piece of emery paper handy when cutting the stencil. Designs were either first drawn in pencil and placed under the heavy waxed stenciling paper or cut directly with the knife. When cutting with a knife, a zinc plate or a piece of glass was placed under the design and stencil paper. Some pupils used a single-edge razor blade instead of a knife.

Although several ways of applying the color have been described, Figure 219b shows the use of a professional stenciling brush. When several stencils were cut, pins or paper tabs were used as guides, as shown in Figure 219b. Guides are important because they keep the stencil paper in the correct position and assure proper register. Other methods of applying paint when using a stencil include atomizers, small garden or household sprayers, airbrushes, and rollers.

Figure 220 shows the stencils which were used by a high school pupil to create the landscape design in Figure 221. To make sure that the correct areas were cut out for each color, the areas were numbered on the original drawing. All the areas to be cut out for the first stencil were marked 1; the second, 2; the third, 3; and finally, the fourth

were marked with a 4. A No. 8 stencil brush was used to stencil this landscape design on regular white drawing paper, using showcard or tempera colors. It can be observed that simple, bold patterns were used.

In most cases it was found best to use only one stencil for each color; sometimes an exception was made. It can be observed in Figure 220, for example, that the lower left-hand stencil was used for the dark green color and yet, the two cross members of the black fence were included. This was done to save stencil paper. It can readily be seen that the black fence in the lower left part

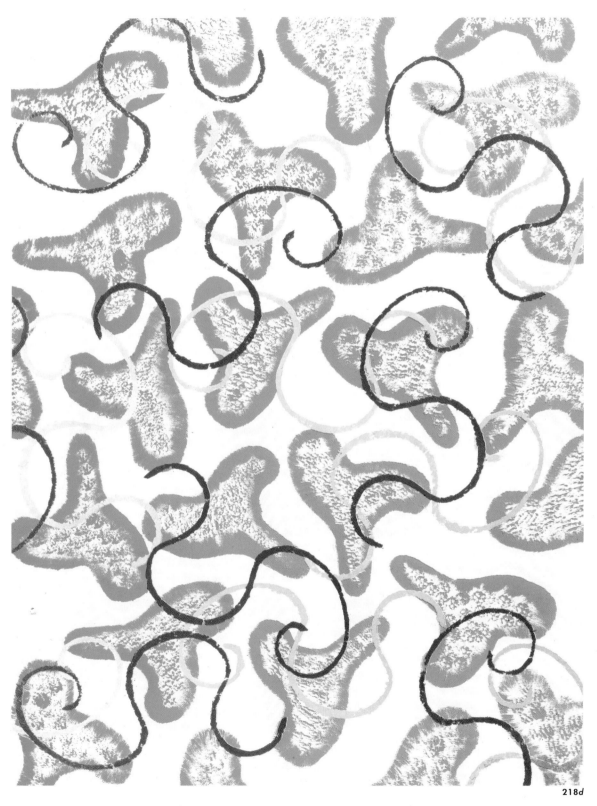

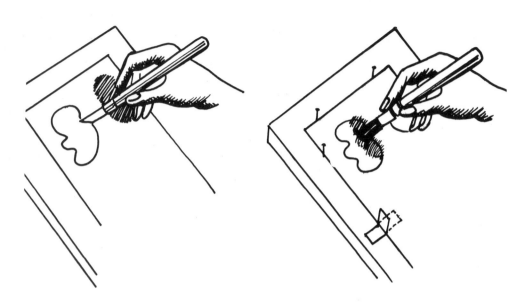

of the picture in Figure 221 had to be made with two stencils. If done on one stencil, the rectangular shapes in the middle of the fence would fall out. Two colors were also used with the lower right stencil in Figure 220. One was the brown color used for the road and sides of buildings and the other was for the blue sky. A three-dimensional effect was achieved by using several colors of different values from light to dark when stenciling a cutout shape.

Stencils used for landscapes and other pictorial designs call for careful planning of simple, bold shapes, proper register, and effective use of colors and values so that the completed pictorial design is pleasing and harmonious. Stenciled pictorial designs make excellent wall decorations, greeting cards, and illustrations for children's books.

Pupils also experimented with stenciling on a

221

222

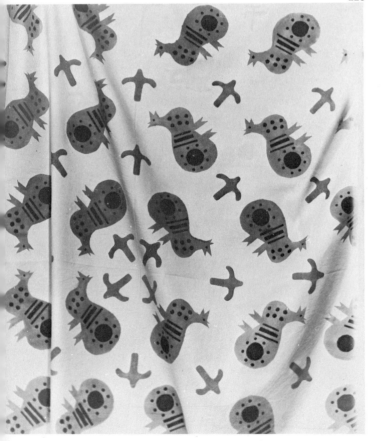

223

variety of fabrics. Figure 222 shows a student stenciling an over-all pattern on a cotton tablecloth. The completed design is shown in Figure 223. The following materials were used for this project: a professional stenciling brush, aluminum pie pans, cotton tablecloth, commercial textile inks, charcoal, string, scissors, and clean rags.

After the pupil had thought out a design which would be suitable for stenciling, she cut out three stencils from aluminum pie pans, using an ordinary pair of pointed scissors. The first stencil was used for the bird, the second for the corn, and the third for the decorative details which were superimposed on the bird design. Guide lines were

put in with charcoal and string to aid in the alignment of the designs when stenciling.

Aluminum stencils were very successful because they were easy to cut and held up very well with use. They could be cleaned quickly since they did not absorb the ink. Thin acetate stencils were also used but did not hold up as well as aluminum.

225

The following is a list of some of the articles that may be stenciled: bookmarks, greeting cards, landscapes, booklets, blotter covers, baskets, portfolios, small folding screens, handbags, cushion covers, curtains, tablecloths, table mats, and laundry bags. Some of the materials which may be stenciled are all kinds of wrapping paper,

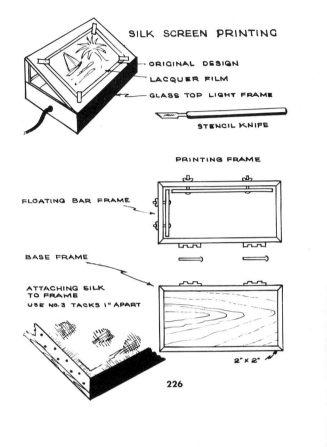

SILK SCREEN PRINTING

ORIGINAL DESIGN
LACQUER FILM
GLASS TOP LIGHT FRAME

STENCIL KNIFE

PRINTING FRAME

FLOATING BAR FRAME

BASE FRAME

ATTACHING SILK
TO FRAME
USE NO. 3 TACKS 1" APART

2" X 2"

226

227

228

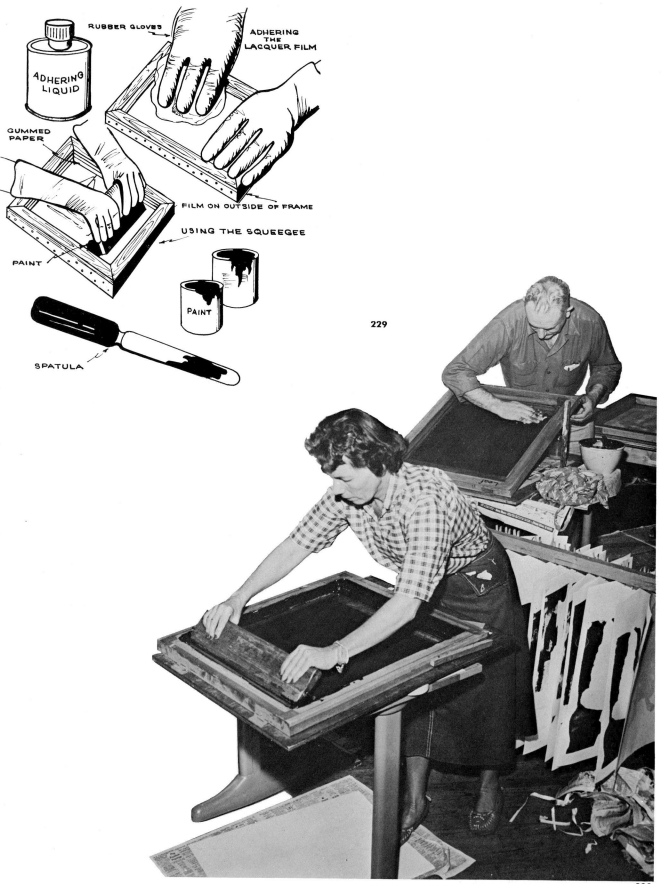

ADHERING LIQUID

RUBBER GLOVES

ADHERING THE LACQUER FILM

GUMMED PAPER

FILM ON OUTSIDE OF FRAME

USING THE SQUEEGEE

PAINT

PAINT

SPATULA

229

230

tinted paper, linen, cardboard, masonite, ply-wood, leather, silk, burlap, oilcloth, aluminum, plastic, tile, canvas, and concrete. Stenciling media may include watercolors, wax crayon, oil paints, dyes, and other commercial preparations.

Since working with stencils has many things in common with serigraphy, the evaluation of pupils' work and a summary will be included at the end of this chapter after some experiments with serigraphy are presented and discussed.

Silk-screen printing, or serigraphy, is a modern form of printing and has become a vast subject. In this chapter we deal with some aspects of it to enable the teacher and reader to get some idea and appreciation of what has been done by students and others with this form of art expression.

231

Pupils at the 3rd grade level experimented with silk-screen printing and found this an exciting way to express their ideas and gain a greater appreciation of design. The materials for their project consisted of 6-inch embroidery hoops, crinoline, Nu-Media paint, an assortment of paper, and scissors.

The 6-inch embroidery hoops with crinoline stretched over them made satisfactory silk-screen frames for young children to work with. With a pair of scissors they cut out paper shapes which were less than 6 inches in size. Next, they arranged the shapes under the silk-screen frame which rested on a sheet of paper and then placed

232

some Nu-Media paint into the frame. Nu-Media paint was used because it is water-soluble and, therefore, easier to clean. Instead of using a squeegee, they used their hands. As they spread the paint, the paper shapes under the frame adhered to the crinoline. The impressions made on the paper on which the frame rested showed that the paper shapes or designs blocked the paint from coming through the crinoline and appeared the color of the paper, as shown in Figure 224. This is the basic principle involved in serigraphy.

Figure 225 is an example of a lower elementary pupil's work showing the background blocked out and the design appearing in color, which is just the opposite of the experiment shown in Figure 224. The prints made interesting wall decorations.

Figure 226 shows how a printing frame was constructed by several junior high school pupils. Pieces of pine, 2 by 2 inches, were used for the frame. Printing frames may have one or two floating bars. The purpose of these bars is to tighten the silk or organdy. For ordinary printing there is no need for these bars if the silk is stretched evenly and tightly and securely fastened with tacks, spaced approximately one inch apart. A base frame, fastened to the printing frame with door hinges, is helpful when printing posters and other similar projects. When printing large surfaces, such as over-all patterns on textiles, the base frame is not used.

Serigraphic silks come in a variety of weaves, each especially prepared for a specific purpose. Organdy may also be used although it is not quite as effective as serigraphic silk.

When the silk was stretched and tacked to the frame, the outside edges were shellacked to help keep the silk in place and prevent the paint from seeping through during printing. Sealing the inside edges with tape also helped. Figure 227 shows the setup used by high school seniors as a class project in printing the toy and mounting board shown in Figure 228.

The top drawing in Figure 226 shows the use of a light frame for cutting lacquer film, a popular method used for printing. In this method the film is placed over a pencil or ink design and cut with a stencil knife. Only the film is cut and not the backing. The cutouts are carefully removed and the stencil is placed, film side up, under the frame and adhering liquid is applied, as shown in the top drawing of Figure 229. The backing of the stencil usually curls up and can be pulled off easily. The adhering liquid softens the film and makes it adhere to the silk. The second drawing in Figure 229 shows the use of a squeegee. Paint is put into the frame with a spatula. Figure 230 also shows the use of the squeegee, as well as a method used to dry prints.

There are many different kinds of lacquer film, as well as paints, for specific types of work and the directions of the manufacturer should be carefully followed. When printing, the frame is raised

233

approximately 1/32 to 1/16 inch away from the object to be printed.

Other methods of silk-screen printing include the block-out method. Such media as glue, shellac, and lacquer are used to block out parts of the design which are not to be printed. Another way is the tusche resist method. There are many other methods as well as combinations of methods. It is only through research and actual participation that an appreciation for silk-screen printing may be developed.

There are many uses for silk-screen work. Figure 231 is an example of a landscape mural called *Intermezzo* while Figure 232 is a different scene called *Panorama*.

Two men usually operate the large squeegee which is used since the murals are approximately 4 by 8 feet. Sometimes a mechanical device is used to pull the squeegee.

Serigraphy is used to make prints for exhibition purposes as shown in Figure 233, entitled *The Wedding Feast at Cana* and Figure 234 entitled *Agnus Dei*. These were made by college students. It is also widely used for printing toy designs, wallpaper, fabrics, posters, advertising displays, reproducing decorations on ceramics, glassware, labels, bottle caps, signs of all kinds, book covers, menus, lampshades, and plastic objects, as well as many others. Silk-screen printing can be done on flat as well as curved surfaces and on as many different kinds of materials as mentioned for stenciling.

In evaluating the stenciling and serigraphic projects made by the pupils, we agreed that although the way a design is carried out is important, the emphasis in evaluation should be placed on how well the individual expressed his ideas, thoughts, or feelings rather than on technical skills. We could admire a pupil's result as an end in itself in terms of how well it was carried out to accomplish the purpose for which it was made.

In summarizing the work done in this chapter it would seem that stenciling and serigraphy projects can be effectively carried on by students from the third grade on through the college level. Both of these methods of printing were fascinating and absorbing experiences for students of practically all age and grade levels. It can be said that methods of stenciling and serigraphy have very much in common. Experimenting with stenciling is a stepping stone toward experimenting in and understanding serigraphy. The basic difference between the two is that in serigraphy the cutout shape or design is covered with a fabric through which the pigment is squeezed by hand or with a squeegee. Both methods are flexible and the great range and variety of techniques which can be developed give the individual much opportunity for creative expression.

Serigraphy, especially, has great value for commercial purposes as well as being a medium for creative expressions which can be used for exhibition purposes in art galleries.

Considerable manipulative skills are developed by using these methods of printing and a greater use, understanding, and appreciation of design is gained by the students.

234

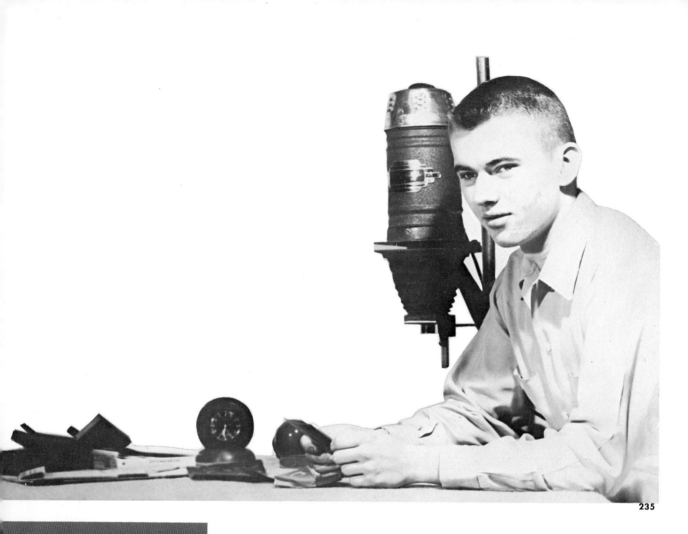

235

Designs Created With Incised Photographic Negatives, (Photograms, Blueprints, Dry Point and Lithography)

Junior and senior high school pupils who were interested in photography discovered that scratched negatives resulted in jet-black lines on the photographs which they developed. This observation led to the discovery of a new way or technique of making prints by scratching or incising lines into an exposed negative and then chemically developing a print in the usual way.

Some of the equipment and materials that were used are shown in Figure 235 and included outdated negatives which were purchased in a pho-

tographic supply shop at reduced prices. Any type of film was used for this method of making prints. The sheet film came in sizes ranging from approximately 2 ¼ by 3 ¼ inches to approximately 8 by 10 inches. Roll film came in sizes as small as 35 mm., and 8 mm. film used for moving pictures was also used. Standard dark room materials and equipment were used to develop the negative, make enlargements, and develop the print. Simple, sharp objects found around the house were all that was needed to scratch out the designs on the negatives. A phonograph needle made a fine clean line, as did a compass point. A penknife or safety razor proved useful for scraping out large areas, and coarse sandpaper was also effective.

The first step in making an incised negative was to open a package of outdated film and simply expose it to the light. The dull, or emulsion, side of the negative was used to draw and scratch the design on. The emulsion layer is very thin; therefore, it did not take much pressure to cut through it. It was not necessary to cut any deeper than the emulsion layer. Pupils made sure that the cutting tools they used were sharp. They practiced with a variety of tools on scrap pieces of film to get an understanding of the advantages and disadvantages of this process. When incising into the film, pupils held the tool as if it were a pen or pencil. After a little practice they soon discovered that the technique of incising and scratching is similar to the one used for pen and ink work or the scratchboard technique. Figure 236 is an example of strokes which pupils practiced to become acquainted with effective ways in which they could express their thoughts and ideas.

After the students learned to make light and dark tones and different kinds of textural effects, they selected simple objects, preferably ones with flat surfaces, and placed them where they were well lighted. Next, they sketched the objects with a pencil on the emulsion or dull side of the film. With their sharp tools they started to scratch and scrape out the objects. Pupils were advised that lines should indicate both surface direction and textural character. Even simple outlines could be very expressive. When they had completed one subject, they experimented with others and worked for variety in both subject and treatment. Experiments were also made with curved strokes, for they are essential in representing rounded objects. Different tools were used to vary the spacing and make strokes of varied sizes. Pupils also learned to work with different values and to shade objects and place cast shadows correctly. They were instructed to be consistent with the light and dark pattern by keeping in mind the angle and direction of light when working. Figures 237, 238, and 239 are some examples of different subjects and textural effects which were produced with this method of making prints.

The pupils were given the following instructions for exposing the negative, using a printing frame as shown in the step-by-step procedure in Figures 240a–j

240a....Remove glass from frame and clean both sides. Replace glass and insert mask which is about ¼ inch smaller all around than your film. Now, hold your film, emulsion, or dull, side up, and place into frame on top of the mask.

240b....In subdued light, place the contact paper on the negative with the emulsion side of the paper down. Blueprint paper may be used as it is inexpensive and easiest to use because no chemicals are necessary to develop the print. Velite may be used not closer than five feet from a 60-watt bulb. When using other contact paper, use a yellow safelight; follow the manufacturers' instructions.

240c....With the mask, film, and paper in place, close the lid of the printing frame. Put away the rest of the printing paper to protect it from exposure to direct light.

236

240d.... Correct exposure of the film to light in making a print requires a little experimentation. When using blueprint paper, expose the frame to sunlight until the shadows turn a bronze color. The print should be washed in running water for ten minutes. Experiment with Velite by using one RFL flood at 16 inches from the negative for four seconds or one No. 1 flood at 8 inches for three seconds. If you use other papers, follow the manufacturers' instructions carefully. Commercial contact printers, which come in different sizes and prices, are available and make work a little easier. If prints larger than the negative are needed, any good quality enlarger may be used. Make sure, however, that you use enlarging paper instead of contact paper.

240e.... After correct exposure, you are now ready to develop the print. Blueprints may be made a deeper and more pleasing blue by first washing the print in the usual way and then placing it for about fifteen minutes in a solution made of 1 ounce of potassium alum and 20 ounces of water. It should then be washed again in pure water. For developing photographic prints, it is suggested that you buy ready-mixed chemicals which include the developer, short-stop, and fixer. All you have to do is pour these chemicals into water and you are ready to develop. It is recommended that the temperature of the first solution which you use, the developer, be 68° F. Mix this solution in the correct proportions in a glass beaker, stir with a stirring rod, and pour into a large glass, hard rubber, or porcelain pan. Slide paper into the developer face up. With a pair of tongs move the paper gently in the solution for approximately one minute.

237

238

240f . . . . Take the package of short-stop which is 1 ½ ounces of 28% acetic acid, and add it to 32 ounces of water. The temperature of the solution should be from 65-70° F. Mix and pour into a large tray. Remove the print from the developer, shake off the excess water, and drop the print into the short-stop, making sure that the developer tongs do not touch the rinse. Agitate the print with the fixer tongs for about 15 seconds.

240g . . . . Now, remove the print from the rinse with the fixer tongs and place in the fixer which you have previously mixed. The temperature of the solution should be from 65-70° F. Agitate the print for approximately 20 minutes or, better still, follow the manufacturers' instructions.

240h . . . . Generally speaking, prints should be washed for an hour in running water, the temperature of the water being between 65° and 70° F. Prints may be washed in a sink basin which has an overflow. To help circulate the water, a hose should be attached to the faucet.

240i . . . . When drying the print, one has to take into consideration whether it should have a matte (non-glossy) finish or a glossy one. For a matte finish, place the washed print in a blotter roll, picture side against the muslin sheet. Roll the blotter, tie up, and leave the print in the blotter roll until dry.

240j . . . . Glossy prints are made with glossy paper. After washing, place prints on a wet ferrotype tin; then cover prints and tin with unprinted newspaper, paper hand toweling, or a clean cloth. Next, firmly apply a roller, back and forth and from side to side. Remove the covering from the prints and let them dry slowly until they peel off. There are numerous electrically heated, drum-type, rotary dryers with canvas covers which do a quicker job of drying the prints.

Designs printed with incised photographic negatives were used to make greeting cards, book plates, and exhibition prints.

Teachers are cautioned to make sure that proper supervision is given to the pupils when working with chemicals in the darkroom. One way which proved successful was to appoint key students to help with the supervision. Usually two or three pupils in the class had quite a bit of experience in developing prints in their own darkrooms at home and were most cooperative in helping to supervise the beginning students. Particular attention was paid to the safety of the pupils and efficient and economical handling of photographic equipment and supplies.

A summary of this project and others described in this chapter will be made at the end of the chapter.

Several pupils in the junior and senior high school also experimented with photograms. This was a simple method of making prints and gave the pupils an opportunity to learn how to make well-balanced designs and how to develop and fix prints.

239

The materials and equipment used included enlarging paper, an enlarger, photographic chemicals, objects of different textures and degrees of transparency, and a darkroom with all standard equipment necessary to develop prints.

This is the way the project was carried out. After selecting several different objects, a student took these to the darkroom. A package of enlarging paper was opened at the proper distance from a colored light and placed on an easel which laid under the lens of an enlarger. The selected objects were then placed on the enlarging paper to form a well-balanced design, and the enlarger switch put on. The paper was exposed to light for the specified time and the light switched off. After the objects were removed from the enlarging paper, the print was developed and fixed in the manner described in the preceding project.

After further experimentation, this method was abandoned in favor of a simpler one in which blueprint paper was used instead of enlarging paper. Blueprint making is one the cheapest and simplest of printing processes. Students in all the grades at the elementary level, as well as junior

240a

240b

240c

240d

240e

240f

240g

240h

240i

and senior high school students, used this method as no chemicals were needed and the prints were permanent.

The materials and equipment which were used included the following: blueprint paper, a desk lamp, running water, a variety of different-textured opaque objects, preferably flat, and a printing frame.

To make a simple print, a pupil opened the printing frame and placed two leaves on the clean glass and then put a piece of blueprint paper, cut to the proper size, over the leaves. The printing

240j

frame was then closed and the paper exposed to sunlight or a desk lamp. The type of desk lamp and printing frame used can be seen in the left-hand portion of Figure 235. The paper was left in the sunlight or under the lamp until the shadows were bronzed, and then it was washed in running water for ten minutes. Figure 241 shows the result of this simple experiment. Blueprints of a deeper shade may be obtained by first washing the print in the above way and then placing it for about fifteen minutes in a solution prepared with 1 ounce of potassium alum and 20 ounces of water. The prints are then washed in running water again.

Elementary grade pupils made reproductions of simple silhouette designs in this way and used them for greeting cards. String and yarn were also used effectively to make unique abstract designs. Pupils enjoyed this project because they experienced a real thrill when they watched the designs emerge when the print was washed in running water. This process shows in a simple, direct, and economical way how a print can be developed. By moving the objects around, the pupils learned how to compose a balanced design. For many students this was their first real experience in developing a skill in printing.

Dry point was another interesting way of creating designs by printing, conducted by students at the college level. This could also be done by students in high school if the materials and equipment are available. Although dry point is usually done on a zinc or copper plate, pupils also experimented by using celluloid or clear plastic sheets. The purpose of this project was to acquaint the pupils with this process of printing which was used by such outstanding artists as Rembrandt, Whistler, and others.

Some of the materials and equipment used were a zinc or copper plate, sheets of celluloid or clear plastic, a grease or china pencil, paper, tarlatan, or unbleached muslin, dry point needle, and an etching press, as shown in Figure 242.

The dry point needle is a slender steel instrument similar to a short pencil sharpened at one end. The first step in getting started was for the students to make some rough pencil sketches to get an idea of the design or composition they planned to carry out. After selecting the best sketch, the pupil drew the design on a prepared plate with a black china pencil. The needle was held in the same manner that a pencil is held and was tilted slightly to one side. In proportion to the pressure used, the dry point needle sank more or less deeply into the metal. It did not, however, cut the plate, but made a furrow which threw up slight, hairlike projections. As the work progressed, a little printers' ink was rubbed into the lines in order to see the design better. The lines varied in quality; some were deep, others shallow, still others narrow, wide, closely placed or crisscrossed, to obtain large masses of dark value.

When a gray tone was desired, the rough edges or projections were removed with a scraper. If, on the other hand, a velvety black tone was sought, the rough hairlike projections were not scraped off. After the edges of the plate were beveled with a file and cleaned with turpentine, the plate was ready for printing.

242

243

A little printers' ink was squeezed on the plate and spread evenly with a small piece of tarlatan and forced into the incised lines. The surplus ink on top of the plate was rubbed off with a piece of unbleached muslin. It was discovered that if the plate was warmed a little on a small electric stove, it was easier to wipe off the ink. A limited number of proofs could be struck off or printed as the process of wiping soon destroys the rough hairlike projections of the furrows.

When all the surface ink was wiped off, ink still remained in the furrows or incised lines. It was this ink that was visible on the paper when the print was struck off. It was observed that, whereas incised lines in a linoleum or wood cut appear white or paper-colored, the lines in the dry point plate appear black on the paper.

A damp, absorbent paper was used when printing. This paper was placed over the design and then covered with a piece of thick flannel. The plate, thus prepared, is placed in the press between two cylinders. The paper between the two cylinders, under considerable pressure, takes up all the ink from the incised lines in the metal plate. When the paper was lifted, as shown in Figure 242, the first proof was made. After that, revisions were made on unsatisfactory parts by either adding or removing lines. Lines were usually

removed by using a scraper which was a three-edged knife and a burnisher which was a piece of polished steel. After each printing, the plate was carefully cleaned and re-inked again. Figure 243 shows a finished print made by a contemporary artist.

For the most part these prints were used as wall decorations or for exhibition purposes.

Although there are many different processes for making prints by incising into a metal plate, dry point was enjoyed by the pupils because it was one of the simplest processes. The results were very satisfying since the dry point process leaves rich, blurry lines that have much beauty in them. This process is not too difficult to grasp and with a little practice pupils found themselves quite familiar with it.

Teachers should emphasize the need and importance of proper storage of the needle. Since this instrument is very sharp, it can inflict considerable harm to the student if proper precautions are not taken. It is also a delicate instrument in the sense that if it is dropped the sharp point may be damaged to the extent that it may become useless.

Students at the college level found lithography to be a fascinating process of printing designs. Although the process was invented in 1796, it has been adapted by many brilliant artists through the years. Besides learning how to use this process, pupils learned to appreciate the different techniques that were used by different artists although the process of printing was basically the same. Students were encouraged to develop their own techniques as soon as they became familiar with this medium.

The materials needed for this project included the following: a stone or a zinc plate, grease pencil or crayon, acid solution, leather-covered roller, paper, and other materials and equipment usually found in an art room.

When experimenting with lithography, the students used a stone, as shown in Figure 244, which also shows several pupils at work on different stages of their designs. Pupils soon learned that the process of making a lithograph is based upon the fact that grease repels water and that oily or fatty substances attract each other.

After the pupil drew his design with a grease pencil or crayon on the stone, it was fixed with a commercially prepared acid solution. A leather-covered roller, impregnated with a greasy ink, was applied over the design. Pupils were reminded to take care to keep the stone moist during the inking. While inking, the pupils observed that the ink adhered to the greasy design but was repelled from the wet background of the stone. When the stone was properly inked, a sheet of paper was placed over the stone and pressed through the lithographic press.

Figure 245 is a finished lithographic print made by a professional artist. It is called *Young Woman*. This print is included in this chapter to show how effectively the artist used large solid areas to form an interesting pattern and express his feeling about the subject.

245

Figure 246 is an unusual print made by a college student. This print has to do with a religious subject and the pupil has expressed his ideas mostly through the use of lines. Some lines are black on a white background while others are white on a black background. A three-dimensional effect or feeling of depth was created by gradually making some of the figures smaller and in this way carrying the eyes farther and farther into the background.

The finished lithographic prints were used as wall decorations or for exhibition purposes.

Pupils found printing with this process a very exciting experience. Working with a grease pencil enabled them to express themselves freely, using a wide variety of subjects and techniques. Pupils sometimes varied the techniques to fit the subject or idea they were expressing.

To summarize some of the activities discussed in this chapter, we learned that one of the simplest ways of making a print is using photographic techniques. Making incised photographic prints was especially suited to help the pupils understand photographic principles and processes in a simple and direct manner. It also helped the pupils to think of photography in terms of an art, with the technique as a means to an end. Emphasis was placed on creative expression, the employment of principles and elements of design toward good composition, and taking into consideration the purpose for which the print is made. Pupils were especially impressed with this printing process because their designs could be reproduced to any desired size with an enlarger. It is hoped that other students will experiment and discover still other ways of using this challenging art medium.

Making photograms, although a fascinating technique, was not as popular as blueprint making. Blueprints had the advantage over photo-grams in that they were more economical and no special equipment or chemicals were absolutely needed. Students at all grade levels could use this method, especially grades 1–6. Students got a real thrill watching their designs emerge as they were washed in clear running water. Using this method, pupils learned a simple and quick way to express some of their ideas; they learned about balanced design and many developed a greater interest in photography.

Students learned that the lines made with dry point, unlike those made in linoleum prints, are the ones which make the black impression on the paper. Dry point prints may be characterized as having rich, blurry lines.

Other processes and variations, in which a zinc or copper plate is used such as etching, soft-ground etching, aquatint, mezzotint, copper engraving, and others where the press forces the paper down onto the inked lines, are not included since these processes are more difficult and require special equipment. A great number of books have been written about these processes and can be readily obtained in any public library by those students who might be interested in pursuing these processes. Some libraries and galleries have picture-lending divisions with excellent examples of these printing processes.

Lithography was discussed to some extent in this chapter to show the pupils another way with which they might express themselves. We learned that lithography differed from printing with lines incised in a metal plate. The basic principle involved in lithography is the fact that a greasy or oily surface repels water and oily substances attract each other.

We learned that although the different processes follow a more or less definite procedure, there is a great deal of opportunity for the students to express themselves in a variety of techniques which would be characteristic of their own personality.

An interesting hobby for students would be to start collecting prints. It is possible to buy a good print by a contemporary artist for a few dollars. A collection may turn out to be a profitable investment if wise choices are made. A young, aspiring artist of today may become a famous master at some future date.

246

BIBLIOGRAPHY

CHAPTER 1

Bean, Philip C., **The Language of Art.** New York: The Ronald Press Company, 1958.

Biddle, George, **The Yes and No of Contemporary Art.** Cambridge, Mass.: Harvard University Press, 1957.

D'Amico, V. E., **Creative Teaching in Art,** rev. ed. Scranton, Pa.: International Textbook Company, 1953.

Downer, Marion, **Discovering Design.** New York: Lothrop, Lee & Shepard Company, Inc., 1947.

Emerson, Sybil, **Design.** Scranton, Pa.: International Textbook Company, 1955.

Ettenburg, Eugene, "Modern Influences on Printing Designs," **American Artist.** New York: Watson-Guptill Publications, Inc., September, 1956.

Faulkner, R. N., and others, **Art Today,** 3d ed. New York: Henry Holt and Company, 1956.

Ford, K. M., and Creighton, T. H., **Designs for Living.** New York: Reinhold Publishing Corporation, 1955.

Graves, M. E., **Art of Color and Design,** 2d ed. New York: McGraw-Hill Book Company, Inc., 1951.

Kaufmann, Edgar, **What is Modern Design?** New York: Museum of Modern Art, 1950.

Moholy-Nagy, L., **Vision in Motion.** Chicago: P. Theobald, 1947.

Pitz, Henry C., "The Design of the Paperback Book," **American Artist.** New York: Watson-Guptill Publications, Inc., March, 1957.

Teague, W. D., **Design This Day,** rev. ed. New York: Harcourt, Brace and Company, 1949.

Trilling, M. B., and Williams, Florence, **Design Your Home for Living.** Philadelphia: J. B. Lippincott Company, 1953.

Winebrenner, D. Kenneth, **Jewelry Making as an Art Expression.** Scranton, Pa.: International Textbook Company, 1955.

CHAPTER 2

Andrews, Michael F., "The Need for a New Interpretation of Creative Education," **N.Y.S.A.T.A. Newsletter.** Binghamton, N. Y.: N.Y.S.A.T.A., January-February, 1957.

Baranski, Matthew (Glenn, B. H., and Smith, C. E., advisers), **Relationship Between Doctoral Degree Programs in Art and Needs of Leaders in Art Education.** Buffalo, N. Y.: University of Buffalo, 1955.

De Francesco, Italo L., **Art Education, Its Means and Ends.** New York: Harper & Brothers, 1958.

Dewey, John, **Art as Experience.** New York: G. P. Putnam's Sons, 1934.

Gaitskell, C. D., **Art Education in the Province of Ontario.** Toronto: Ryerson Press, 1948.

Gaitskell, C. D., and Gaitskell, M. R., **Art Education During Adolescence.** Toronto: Ryerson Press, 1954.

Hagan, Estelle H., and Christensen, Ethel M., **Children's Art Education.** Peoria, Ill.: Charles A. Bennett Company, Inc., 1957.

Hopkins, L. Thomas, **The Emerging Self in School and Home.** New York: Harper & Brothers, 1954.

Kainz, L. C., and Riley, O. L., **Exploring Art.** New York: Harcourt, Brace and Company, 1948.

Lindstrom, Miriam, **Children's Art.** Berkeley, Calif.: University of California Press, 1957.

Long Island Art Teachers' Association, **Art Education in Modern Elementary Schools.**

Lowenfeld, Viktor, **Your Child and His Art.** New York: The Macmillan Company, 1954.

New York State Education Department, **Art Education—An Outline of the Scope and Content of the Art Program in the Early Secondary Grades.** Albany, N. Y.: Bureau of Secondary Curriculum Development, New York State Education Department.

Osborn, Alex, **Wake Up Your Mind.** New York: Charles Scribner's Sons, 1952.

Reed, Carl, **Early Adolescent Art Education.** Peoria, Ill.: Charles A. Bennett Company, Inc., 1957.

School Arts. (All articles pertaining to philosophy and theory of art and graphic designs. A careful study was made in the past several years to gain some understanding and appreciation of trends in contemporary art.) Worcester, Mass.: Davis Publications, Inc.

"The Art Number," **Education,** vol. 77 (all articles). Hingham, Mass.: The Palmer Company, November, 1956.

Title, Irving, "Theory and Practice in Art," **Journal of the National Art Education Association.** Kutztown, Pa.: State Teachers College, February, 1953.

Wickiser, Ralph K., **An Introduction to Art Education.** Yonkers, N. Y.: World Book Company, 1957.

CHAPTER 9

Lord, Lois, **Collage and Construction in Elementary and Junior High School.** Worcester, Mass.: Davis Publications, Inc., 1958.

Murphy, Corrine, **Exploring the Hand Arts.** Girl Scouts, 1955.

Todd, Jessie, "Attractive Materials," **Everyday Art.** Sandusky, Ohio: American Crayon Company, September-October, 1952.

CHAPTER 14

Bliss, Douglas P., **Wood Engraving.** New York: E. P. Dutton and Company, Inc., 1928.

Corbin, Thomas J., **Hand Block Printing on Fabrics.** New York: Pitman Publishing Corporation, 1934.

Kafka, Francis J., **Linoleum Block Printing.** Bloomington, Ill.: McKnight & McKnight Publishing Company, 1955.

Kandinsky, Wassily, **On the Spiritual in Art.** New York: Solomon R. Guggenheim Museum, 1946.

Mueller, H. A., **How to Make Woodcuts and Wood Engravings.** American Artists Group, 1945.

Newick, John, **Making Color Prints; An Approach to Lino Cutting.** Peoria, Ill.: Charles A. Bennett Company, Inc., 1952.

CHAPTER 15

Brownley, Albert, **How to Paint and Stencil Textiles,** 4th ed. Alby Studio, 1952.

Stephenson, J. B., **From Old Stencils to Silk Screening.** New York: Charles Scribner's Sons, 1953.

CHAPTER 16

Dehn, A. A., and Barrett, L. L., **How to Draw and Print Lithographs.** New York: Tudor Publishing Company, 1950.

Eastman Kodak Company, **How to Make Good Pictures.** New York: Random House, 1957.

Geiser, Bernard (introduction), **Pablo Picasso Lithographs 1945-1948.** Valentin, 1948.

Kistler; Aline, **Understanding Prints.** Association of American Artists, 1936.

Sternberg, Harry, **Modern Methods and Materials of Etching.** New York: McGraw-Hill Book Company, Inc., 1949.

Watson, Ernest W. (edited by Norman Kent with introduction by Karl Kup), **Relief Prints.** New York: Watson-Guptill Publications, 1945.

West, Levon, **Making an Etching.** New York: Thomas Y. Crowell Company, 1932.

INDEX